ENDORSE

God's heart for children is that they would be powerful, confident, and equipped to fulfill the mission He has given them of bringing Heaven to Earth. Amy's book is full of helpful instructions and tools that will especially help parents as well as children's ministry leaders to partner with God to raise such children. I encourage you to read the book, follow the instructions, use the tools, and watch what God does with and through your children. Get ready, you may be in for some surprises!

HEATHER THOMPSON
Founder & International Director, Powerpack Ministries,
Aldershot, UK

Often today, we teach a series or share ideas from a popular author with the goal of learning something fresh and anointed. If we want to see any of what we've learned become part of our corporate church culture, it has to show up in the lives of our children. Amy Gagnon is an expert in training our children to believe, understand, and practice a supernatural, Kingdom culture. Her new book, *Raising Powerful Children*, is the outline to equipping our children to need and expect a Gospel of power. Jesus said that He would build the Church, but we are to spread the Kingdom. Built into spreading the Kingdom is a lifestyle that we want each of our children to understand as normal Christianity. This book will help parents, leaders, and children's ministry workers create a path that leads our kids to show the world who Jesus is by training them up in the way that they should go. I wholeheartedly recommend

Raising Powerful Children to anyone with the responsibility to show our children the Gospel of love and power.

Danny Silk
President, Life Academy, El Dorado Hills, CA

If you are reading this, you have found gold! This book is a resource for life. Raising our kids to be healthy and powerful is every parent's dream. Learn how to raise your kids in truth and love and how to connect them to the Father's heart. Amy is an incredible woman, mother, wife, and leader. Although naturally gifted in this area, she has loads of experience. In these pages, you will find truths, encouragement, and activations to help you in *Raising Powerful Children*.

Candace Johnson
Senior Pastor, Studio Church, Greenville, SC

If you are looking for practical wisdom on the subject of raising children to reach their full God-given potential and identity, you've found it with *Raising Powerful Children*. There is unique treasure to be mined in all of our children, and I would invite you to dive into the beautiful mysteries that each of our children hold. Amy's perspective, experience, and expertise make her an outstanding voice to have as your mentor in raising your own children. The investment of the practical followed by the invitation into spiritual development is one of the powerful strengths I've witnessed Amy cultivate for years in her own family, with her four children, as well as in our church and community. This book is timely and will become an incredibly valuable resource for you and your children.

BEN ARMSTRONG
Prophetic Ministry Director, Bethel Church, Redding, CA

RAISING POWERFUL CHILDREN

RAISING POWERFUL CHILDREN

*Training Your Children to Walk
in the Supernatural Power of God*

AMY GAGNON

DESTINY IMAGE® PUBLISHERS, INC.

P.O. Box 310, Shippensburg, PA 17257-0310

"Promoting Inspired Lives."

This book and all other Destiny Image and Destiny Image Fiction books are available at Christian bookstores and distributors worldwide.

Cover design by Eileen Rockwell

Interior design by Terry Clifton

For more information on foreign distributors, call 717-532-3040.

Reach us on the Internet: www.destinyimage.com.

ISBN 13 TP: 978-0-7684-5789-6

ISBN 13 eBook: 978-0-7684-5790-2

ISBN 13 HC: 978-0-7684-5792-6

ISBN 13 LP: 978-0-7684-5791-9

For Worldwide Distribution, Printed in the U.S.A.

1 2 3 4 5 6 7 8 / 25 24 23 22 21

CONTENTS

FOREWORD

IF WE DON'T LIVE INTENTIONALLY, WE WILL BE INFLUENCED and controlled by the culture around us. This truth becomes particularly evident in parenting. If we are going to raise children who will impact the world, we must deliberately instill kingdom values within them. Amy Gagnon's book, *Raising Powerful Children*, aims to clarify kingdom values, raise our expectancy for our children's spiritual life, and equip adults to intentionally sow seeds of truth into the hearts of young people. We carry the mandate of heaven to replicate and demonstrate what God's world is like, and nowhere is that more evident than in the raising of our children.

Our goal at Bethel has been to nurture children who will shape the world. Children naturally dream of greatness. They pretend they are superheroes, running around the house with capes on to save the day. They gravitate toward a God-given dream of significance. But it's our job, as parents and caregivers, to define what greatness in God's kingdom truly is. We plant seeds of significance into the heart of every child, recognizing their emerging gifts and talents without trying to control the destiny of their lives. We speak words of affirmation, lend support, and choose to empower each child so that they can learn to be strong and capable in their area of gifting.

David intentionally parented Solomon, guiding his life when he was a small child. Solomon tells us this in Proverbs 4:3-5:

> *When I was my father's son, tender and the only one in the sight of my mother, he also taught me, and said to me: "Let your heart retain my words; Keep my commands, and live. Get wisdom! Get understanding!"*

David prepared Solomon for his destiny while he was still a child. Then God gave Solomon the chance to have anything he wanted. This is the only time we have a record of this kind of an opportunity being given to anyone. In my opinion, God gave him a choice because he was the only one who had been prepared to make the right choice.

Each chapter in *Raising Powerful Children* is filled with Amy's firsthand experience not only as a leader in children's ministry, but also as a loving parent. She brings insight, encouragement, and practical wisdom to these pages. She shares powerful testimonies of children encountering God in unique ways alongside practical tips for building a kingdom culture within the home. This book is a valuable tool for every person involved in educating and nurturing the next generation. It is never too late to develop a place of influence in the lives of your children and grandchildren.

May every child in your life know the goodness of God. May they be given a heart to know Him as their God and be known as His children as they share their whole heart with Him (see Jer. 24:7).

BILL JOHNSON
Bethel Church, Redding, CA
Author of *Born for Significance* and *Raising Giant-Killers*

INTRODUCTION

In this manner, therefore, pray: Our Father in heaven, hallowed be Your name. Your kingdom come. Your will be done on earth as it is in heaven. Give us this day our daily bread. And forgive us our debts, as we forgive our debtors. And do not lead us into temptation, but deliver us from the evil one. For Yours is the kingdom and the power and the glory forever. Amen.
—MATTHEW 6:9–13

I WROTE THIS BOOK ABOUT CHILDREN WITH A FOCUS ON families in their homes during the 2020 Covid-19 pandemic. My goal in writing this book is to underscore the importance of families and children, and especially the spiritual growth of children. The spiritual development of any person is that individual's responsibility, but parents have been gifted their children from God and bear great responsibility in their children's physical, emotional, and spiritual development. Psalm 127:3–5a says, *"Behold, children are a heritage from the Lord, the fruit of the womb is a reward. Like arrows in the hand of a warrior, so are the children of one's youth. Happy is the man who has his quiver full of them."*

As a children's pastor in the Church, I have seen the majority of families depend on the Church to raise their children spiritually. I am not saying there is a problem with the Church leading children spiritually. I am, though, noticing that parents do not know how to lead, teach, or walk with their children in a relationship with their Heavenly Father. For me, this is a great concern because we could lose generations as a result.

I want to lend my knowledge, heart, and strength to parents on how their "home" or family unit should be the very first place to build the foundation for strong, spiritually connected children who know who they are, know to whom they belong, and know what authority has been given to them. Though I will not be solely focusing on families in this book, they will be the subject of the greater part of our discussion.

I have written this book for parents, but I do want to help the Church as well. I will have a few chapters aimed at those who work with children's ministry in the Church at the end of this book. I want *Raising Powerful Children* to help shift our mindset of children and their connection to Jesus.

If you are not a parent or someone who is running a children's ministry, I want you to know the pages that follow are also for you. The reason why this book is just as important for you as it is for someone in ministry with children is that, most likely, you are connected to a child in one way or another. You may be a grandparent, aunt, uncle, coach, neighbor, teacher, or childcare worker, for example, and the information shared in this book applies to all those similarly connected to a child or to children. In fact, you were once a child, and even that makes this book applicable to your life.

My heart is for children and for healthy, thriving families. It is what I love and give my time and energy toward. I was born into a church plant and was the first baby in its nursery. I know now that being the first baby in a church plant played a very significant role in my life. I had my full circle moment when I realized I was born into something that has defined a big part of my life. To me, working with children feels like an inherited calling.

My passion for children and their connection to Jesus has grown exponentially over the years. I have always loved the Church and have always been drawn to children's ministry. I even have a degree in children's ministry. And then my husband and I had our own children—four girls! Also, for the past sixteen years and counting, I have been involved in children's ministry and am now running a ministry of a few thousand children. My passion is part of my destiny and purpose here on this earth. With each stage of life, I have grown in my passion for children to know and find their connection to Jesus.

When I became a mother and was involved in children's ministry, I found that I had to grow my responsibility to my children and their connection to their Heavenly Father a bit more seriously. I had to start practicing what I taught in the classroom. Coming from a family in the ministry, I understood the importance of bringing what you believe to be true into your home and not just practicing it one or two days a week in church. At times, pastors and ministry leaders live double lives. They are one person for the congregation and a completely different person within the walls of their homes. I knew from the beginning that I had to live what I taught or believed in front of my children. So, when I taught children that they are powerful and what they believe can change the world, I had to figure out with them how that practically plays out in their everyday lives. Often, I have encountered too many people who have been hurt by the hypocrisy of Christian leaders—hypocrisy that they ascribe to the Church or Christianity as a whole. In reality, hypocrisy is a result of the inconsistencies of individuals and not the Church or Christianity. People who are not perfect by nature have misunderstood the true nature of God and have not translated God's heart well to each other.

If there is anything I can do for my children, it is to talk about who God is to me and who God says that He is. Additionally, I let my children know I don't know everything that there is to know about God. My children need to know that life with God is going to take a lifetime to discover. I explain to them that it will take me my whole life to discover all that I can about who God is. I also need to let my children know that I am not perfect and, like them, I am on a journey to discover God. I have been on this journey since I was a small child, and I still have not fully found all of God's heart and love. In fact, I will not know the fullness of God until I enter into my eternal life with Him. Just as this is for me, so it is for them.

This is my commitment to my children—to teach them as much as I know and to learn from them as much as they know. As Pastor Bill Johnson says, my gift to my children is "my ceiling is their floor." The wisdom and experience I can pass onto to my children are an inheritance. My children then can stand upon my life's gift, and they can build beyond what was given to them.

My hope is that you will be able to read each chapter and find some inspiration and hope for your family's journey into the heart of the Father. I have included Scripture, lessons from my journey, testimonies of what God has done with some of my friends, and activations for you to try in your homes—all with the goal of helping you raise powerful children. I encourage you to do this together as a family and not go through your journey with God without each other. When you can come together as a family and seek and find God and discover the depths of His love and heart for each one of you, then you will see many different facets of Him in each other. You will see more because you are including other members in your home, thus helping you to see each other's process and individual walks with God. When you can do this together, you will broaden your awareness of Him through different perspectives.

My children along with my husband and myself have looked at each other and God so differently because we have done this together. What I have experienced with God is not what my husband experiences with God. The same is true with my children. They come from the same gene pool but are very different from each other. The same is true in our experience and relationship with God. For example, my children have asked questions about a verse in the Bible that I would have never thought of on my own, and it caused me to look at the verse completely differently. What they hear from a Scripture may not be what I am hearing when I read the very same Scripture. In my family, we each have been impacted by the members of our family in choosing to do this journey together. We only have our children in our homes for around 20 percent of their lives. I would rather choose to do this together as long as possible before my children become adults and have to do this on their own. If this is done well together, then when they get to do life on their own, they should have a great foundation of who they are and who God is in them.

My prayer is that every family will thrive in growing spiritually together. My heart is that this book will bring you together, stronger in connection, and will cause you to grow in learning more about God and more about each other because God has placed your family together for a reason. God chose you to be connected together by placing you in your family. The beauty with God is that He gives us the choice to be connected beyond placing us together. The goal is to enjoy each other and not feel overwhelmed by life. I encourage you to invite God the Father, Jesus your

Savior, and the Holy Spirit your Counselor into your home and into the lives of your children. I cannot wait to hear what God will do in your homes and families as a result.

Chapter 1

MINISTRY IN YOUR HOME

*Jesus answered and said to him, "If anyone
loves Me, he will keep My word; and My
Father will love him, and We will come to
him and make Our home with him."*
—JOHN 14:23

ONE EVENING WHILE IN MY NEW HOME WITH MY TWO-YEAR-old and six-month-old daughters, we were playing on the floor in their room. Suddenly, my two-year-old looked up at me and asked, "Who is the man standing behind you in the doorway?"

Terror filled my body as I thought there was an intruder in my home. We were the only three home as my husband was out of town on a trip. I slowly turned around, and to my relief, no one was standing there in the doorway leading into the hall. I turned back toward my daughter and said to her, "There is no one there."

"Yes, Mom, there is. Who is that man?"

Trying to figure out what she was seeing, my mind finally thought she could be seeing an angel. "Is the man you see a good man or a bad man?" I asked her.

She replied quickly with a smile, "He is a good man."

"Is he an angel?"

"No! Mommy, He is Jesus!"

Tears filled my eyes as I immediately felt the presence of God fill our room and home. From this point forward, our daughter continued to "see" angels, Jesus, and eventually demonic beings in our home. I realized I had to figure out how to help her and spiritually lead her. The problem I faced was I could not relate to or understand what she was experiencing. It had not been my experience as a child. So, I found a lady who worked for me at my church, knowing that she had "seen" things in the spirit realm since she was a child. I asked her what she thought would have been helpful to her as a child and how I could help my daughter with what she was experiencing. What I learned was very helpful.

My friend first informed me that I just needed to believe that what my daughter was experiencing was real. This was foundational to build trust in my daughter's journey. I actually understood what my friend was saying to me because my first thoughts and feelings were fearful as I could not relate to my daughter. And I had been concerned that maybe she was making it all up. I also learned that the peace, love, and fear I experienced that evening in my children's room were evident and very real to my daughter even though she was only two years old.

This experience with my daughter was the beginning of our journey in our parent and child relationship. It was the beginning of my helping steward this reality for her and in leading, encouraging, empowering, and speaking truth to her in this part of her life. She needed someone to help her figure out what to do with this gift of seeing in the spirit realm.

Honestly, my husband and I do not know why she has this gift, but she does. We know that God is the giver of gifts and she has a responsibility to do something with her gift. To be clear, this has been a journey of experimentation. It has not been something that I or my husband have been very familiar with, but we do know that angels, Jesus, and the demonic encounters are in God's Word. So, hers was a gift and not a burden.

I believe we need to make sure our homes are places in which we can build and raise powerful children. Our children are gifts to us from the Lord, and God chose us to be the parents who lead and raise them. We have the authority to lead our children, and many times families depend on the Church to be the only source of leadership or the only role models to develop our children's spiritual lives. Please hear me out. I love the Church, and the Church does have a role to play in the spiritual lives of our children, but we as parents need to realize we are the first and foremost leaders in developing our children. We need to discover who our children are, meaning who they are to God and why they have been put on this earth in our homes. And then we need to steward our time with them well.

Jesus died for us, and when He left this earth, we were given the Spirit of God to guide and counsel us. As parents, we have the best Guide and Counselor known to Heaven and Earth. It is the Spirit of the Living God, the Spirit of the Creator of Heaven and Earth living among us. The Spirit of God is here for us to have access to counsel and to seek help and guidance. The payment has been paid, and all you have to do is lay down your life, acknowledge that Jesus died for your life, and then you can call Him your King and Savior.

When you are raising your children, you need to have one ear to your child or children and one ear to Heaven. You need to ask the Holy Spirit to help you understand your child or children. We are not alone in this journey as parents. God created and formed your children while they were in the womb, and He knows the very design of who you have in your home. God knows why He uniquely created them. I am always amazed at just how unique our children are. If you were to have a dozen children that came from the same two people and gene pools, you still would have twelve very different people. It honestly amazes me how different children are from one another and from their parents, for that matter. They are not a stamp of the previous sibling or a stamp for the one who comes after them. They can look differently, think differently, process differently, learn differently, and respond differently. It is truly amazing!

There are several different influences impacting our children. If we depend on the influences outside our homes, then those influences will guide and raise our children. Whether we want that to happen or not, it will happen. We cannot be afraid of the world. In 1 John 4:4, we read, *"You are of God, little children, and have overcome them, because He who is in you is greater than he who is in the world."* If we are raising powerful children, then we must let them be powerful. Many times, parents are so worried about the world that we shelter or hide our children, and they never become powerful. Our children will need to be empowered to become powerful, and this is a journey that we do not accomplish overnight. We should start as early as we can, and the goal is to teach our children who they are, not who they should not be.

I am reminded of a story a friend told me when she managed a bank. She said that bank tellers are trained with real money. They learn about all the markings, the type of paper, the hidden images, and the different fibers that make up real money. They never handle or study counterfeit money. The reason being, if they study counterfeit money, then they can confuse the counterfeit with the real money. Studies have shown that, if you only study the real money, then you can easily identify the counterfeit. This is true with how we raise our children. We should not focus on what the world is telling us that real love, happiness, and success look like. We should tell our children what God says about all of these in His Word, because His Word is what is real and true.

Our children not only need to hear truths in our homes, but they need to learn how to practically apply those truths in their lives, and we need to do the same as parents, too. Be as real and authentic as possible with your children. If you do not know the answers to certain questions, then let your children hear you say, "Gosh, I am not sure yet. What I do know, though, is that God knows all the answers and He wants us to ask Him."

Empowering your children to be powerful is really giving them opportunities to practice being powerful. Give them opportunities from the earliest age to pray, to worship, to prophesy, to declare, to ask God what He is saying or doing, and to engage with God in different ways. This is true even in your home. We should be doing things together for the sake of learning, and we should be learning from each other.

Remember, for example, if your children watch you cook them food, it does not mean they know how to cook food themselves. You would need to teach them the why and the how and let them try. There are different times in their lives where it would be more appropriate to do certain tasks in cooking than others. If they're really young, then they can mix or measure cold ingredients in a bowl while being supervised. Once they get older and more capable, they might be able to cut up vegetables or cook on the stovetop or in the oven. The same application is true spiritually as we raise our children.

Not every spiritual opportunity is appropriate at every stage of life, but as they grow you can see how they handle each stage of learning and growing. Growth should be in the mindset, and what I mean is that there should always be opportunities to grow. If your child is not growing, then find different ways to help them grow. Your children cannot grow in cooking if they are only measuring and mixing cold ingredients. Another way to look at it would be, let them measure cold ingredients, then let them mix cold ingredients. Later, let them turn on the burner, then let them pour the ingredients in a pan on the stove and cook them. The next stage would be to clean up the kitchen and put things away. Lastly, let them have full range of the kitchen with a recipe and let them cook the whole meal and clean up by themselves without your assistance but with your availability to help if need be. This process has growth in mind. There is always room to add more to their skillset, and eventually they will be able to do everything from start to finish without you.

You want your children to leave your home capable, knowing who they are and who God is before they leave. Honestly, we will never know God fully, but knowing who they are and who He is as much as possible before leaving your home is the goal. The goal is not their knowing as much as you know but for them to *exceed* your knowledge and awareness. You as a whole family will even grow in your knowledge and understanding of who you are and who God is because you are doing this together. There is always growth, and this does not just apply to your children. Knowing that each moment, each conversation, and each encounter can cause us to learn more about ourselves and God is really beautiful!

Learning about ourselves and God should be natural and not forced. It is as simple as having discussions with your children as you go about your daily tasks. You may go on a walk, and your children may ask why the sky is blue. Explaining the scientific answers is great but always adding God into the subject is the goal. You can add creation into the conversation and even ask God together what He was thinking when He created the universe. Then ask your children what they hear God saying in response. They may or may not give you the answers, but you are teaching them about the journey of life where it is natural and good to ask God and hear what He is saying to us. At least reading about creation in God's Word regarding the stages of creation shows your children to go to the source first.

ACTIVATION

Journaling is a great practice. Here are some things you can journal about:

1. Take some time to ask God who your children are to Him.

2. What is God saying to you about your children?

3. What are the things your children are interested in?

4. Do they like worship or talking about God's Word?

5. Have they heard His voice?

6. Do they want their friends and family to know what they know?

7. Do they like to write, color, or paint when they learn?

8. Do they like to tell others about what God is saying?

9. Can they feel God?

10. What do they say He feels like?

11. Have your children start a journal about their discovery with God:

- Have them write down about a time they have experienced God.

- Have them journal a truth they have discovered.

- Have them write down a testimony of something God has done for them.

- Have them journal when someone has ministered to them.

- Have them write down a prophetic word or a Bible verse someone has given them.

Have fun discovering who you have in your home and letting them discover who God is to them. Children growing into who God has intended them to be and your family growing into who you all are meant to be as a family are great accomplishments. I pray this would be a beautiful journey of discovery and growth. When your children look back, they can read about what you, their parents, said about them and what God has done in their lives. It will be powerful!

Chapter 2

CHILDREN MUST HAVE THEIR OWN RELATIONSHIPS WITH GOD

Good things as well as bad, you know, are caught by a kind of infection. If you want to get warm you must stand near the fire: if you want to be wet you must get into the water. If you want joy, power, peace, eternal life, you must get close to, or even into, the thing that has them. . . . They are a great fountain of energy and beauty spurting up at the very center of reality. If you are close to it, the spray will wet you: if you are not, you will remain dry.
—C.S. LEWIS, *Mere Christianity*

ONE DAY A LITTLE THREE-YEAR-OLD BOY, WHO WAS A REGU-lar attendee at our church, came into one of our classrooms with a Lego figurine sword. As you can imagine, it was very small. Our teacher immediately placed it in an envelope because of its size and because she knew it was valuable to this little guy. She did not want it to get lost, and she planned to hand it back to his mother when the class was over.

Well, both the teacher and child forgot about the sword, weeks and eventually months went by. Finally, one morning, the teacher remembered as the mother checked her son into the class. She told the mom that she had the little sword for months and wanted to give it to her so she would not forget it again. Immediately, the mother of this boy started to cry. She started to explain to the teacher with tears running down her cheeks that her son had been looking for this toy sword for the past several months. The mother said that, finally, the night before the class, he had come running out of his room and said God told him that tomorrow his Sunday School teacher would give it to them. The mother thought what her son said was "cute" but did not realize until the moment the teacher handed this toy sword to her that morning at church that God had actually spoken to her son and that her son had heard God speaking. It moved her and changed the way she saw her son.

Children must learn to have their own connection and relationship with God. Parents and leaders must model great relationships with the Father, but many times children are just assumed to have a relationship with God because they are brought to church, they attend a Christian school, their parents are Christians, etc. Assumptions do not count in the Kingdom of God. Jesus demonstrated many examples of coming into relationship with God the Father. The one assumption many parents make is that, if they bring their children to church, church will walk their children through the relationship. Hearing teaching at church is one way children can hear about the salvation of Jesus and can expose them to the truth. This works for some children. The problem, though, is we are looking at salvation as fire insurance against hell. We need to reveal the Father to our children as a relationship for life.

Our job as parents is to take our children to the Father's hand and let them have their own connection and relationship with Him. A great way to start is by example. In many of my chapters in this book, I will show you how to connect to who children are in God's design, and I will show you how to have them connect to God Himself. Children must know who they are in Christ, know who God is, know how to connect to Him, and know how God wants to use them in their lives. With these four keys of foundational knowledge and understanding, I think we are doing more for them and their spiritual lives than if all we ensure they did was say a prayer of salvation. God wants us to know Him deeply, and He wants to be invited into every area of our lives.

As you recall in the introduction of this book, I shared that I grew up in church yet I did not fully know God for myself. To be honest, my relationship with God is one of constant discovery. I find out new things about Him and my own identity in Him each day. We are not going to know the fullness of God in our walk on this earth, but we should do our best to get to know Him. And when it comes to our children's spiritual lives, we want to connect them to Him as soon as we possibly can.

I was in college when I discovered the person of the Holy Spirit for the first time. Growing up, the Holy Spirit was someone I heard about from the book of Acts. I was never taught He was supposed to be a part of my life just as much as He was a part of the believers' lives in the book of Acts. This season of my life shifted so much of my awareness of God. I realized that there was more to discover about Him and His Kingdom. It was another facet to the Deity of God, but also in my discovery of Him I found out more about who I was and how I responded to this new person. It broadened my relationship and understanding of God and myself. Right then, I vowed to myself that my children would know God the Father, Jesus the Son of God, and the Holy Spirit our Counselor and Guide. I chose then and there to help lead my children into their own discovery from my personal discovery.

There can be a time when your children will ride your coattails of relationship with God. They may even ride your coattails of faith. There should be, however, an *"and then"* in their walk, like learning to walk without your hands holding them up. This is when they experience the fullness of God the Father, Jesus the Son, and the Holy Spirit for themselves. The wholeness of God may be someone they hear about, but there should be an *"and then"* when they experience the Godhead. This makes the lives of our children come to a place of life flowing in and out of them. This is their journey of discovery even if what they're experiencing comes as a result of witnessing the life of a great example.

If you are a parent, it is important to realize that God chose you to be the parent to your children for a reason. I cannot think of my children without thinking of the word *legacy*. To me, a legacy is something I am leaving to my children. For me, it is something that does not die with me but lives on beyond myself and even beyond ensuing generations. I want my children to take what I have given them not just in value, but in values and character, and then add to that. When they take what I have given them, what I have laid my life down with them in mind and handed to them, then they themselves may add to this, resulting in compound interest in their lives and in the lives of their children. They can pass this very same approach on to their children. This can go on and on when instilled well into your children.

God is eternal, and His design is eternal. When I think of this concept of legacy, I think it can be an eternal concept if it is picked up by the next generation and they themselves add to it. You were chosen by God to create legacy in your family. Again, this is the idea that "our ceiling is their floor." We get to create legacy whether we know it or not. Our children can be given something amazing, or they may be given something that does not produce life. There are many times we all have said, "I will never raise my children the way my parents raised me." However, you can decide to change how you parent by not parenting like your parents did or by taking some great nuggets of wisdom in how your parents raised you as a kind of legacy and choosing to deposit it along with your own knowledge, wisdom, and values in your children.

This relationship with God starts with you. Your homes should be the center of your connection with God and your children's connection with God. The Church should be the reinforcement of connection with God. Without my church, family, Christian school, and community, my children would not have had reinforcement. I am so thankful for the people who came around my children, my husband, and myself and instilled value and connection to God. Without them, I am not sure I would have the same children who have hearts connected to who they are, connected to who God is, and connected to how God wants to use them in their lives. It really does take a village to reinforce these values and concepts.

Our lives at home should be the most authentic and real places to model our connections. I am not saying our homes have to be perfect because that is not real or attainable. But our homes must be real and authentic, though. So many times, I have gone to God messy, and my children have watched me walk out my messiness. I think messiness with an honoring posture is freeing for others to watch. I remember one such time when our dog's foot was broken in a freak accident in our home. In that moment, I clearly did not model my connection to God. I say "clearly" because my daughter saw my face. It said that I was immediately frustrated and angry. She stopped me in that moment and told me that it was going to be okay. She encouraged me to pray for God to help and heal our dog. She was able to come to me, her mother, in that moment and speak hope and truth. She addressed the messiness of my emotions and knew I could be better at how I was approaching this moment.

She knew she could do this because she saw me in a better posture before. We live out our process with God for our children to see, including the best of us and the not-so-best parts of us.

ACTIVATION

1. Start collecting things like art supplies, worship cloths, or Bibles for your children.

2. Place what you've collected for each child in a basket or bin.

3. Make a special spot in your home to rest with God.

-   Make a tent in your children's room to talk to God.

-   Have a special blanket that is designated for your time with God.

-   Have your children help create this space.

-   Make this space special for you and your children.

-   Let your children know they can bring their basket or bin with them in this space.

-   Make sure you have a space as well in the same space or in a different space.

Chapter 3

NO JUNIOR HOLY SPIRIT

But you shall receive power when the Holy Spirit has come upon you; and you shall be witnesses to Me in Jerusalem, and in all Judea and Samaria, and to the end of the earth
—ACTS 1:8

DURING AN EVENING SERVICE IN OUR FOUR-YEAR-OLD CLASS-room, our team was getting to the end of the service time. The evening services at our church can last up to four hours, and our children are in the classrooms that entire time. Our team had gone through worship, the lesson, crafts, and games, and they were then at a point that they wanted to put on a video to entertain the children. One team member could not settle for a video, however. The rest of the team decided that these children were able to watch videos at home, and they recognized the moment could be used to help the children experience more of God. Our team did not know what exactly they should do, so they decided to walk around and pray for

God to show them what to do with the children. One team member decided to pray in the Spirit and realized that some of the children might not know what she was doing. She then started to pray for God to show the children how to pray in the Spirit.

In the next few minutes following her prayer, God started to move in the room with the children. Children started to pray in a language they never heard before, and some children felt God's presence fall over them in a way they have never felt before. Others felt the weight or glory of God in the room and could not move. Children were experiencing a move of His Spirit over them. Twenty to thirty minutes into this moment, their parents started to come to the door, and then they began to watch their children experience the Spirit of God. This led to the parents feeling the Spirit of God moving over them. I believe that God's Spirit was sent here to teach us, but what we witnessed that evening was similar to the move over believers in the book of Acts.

That moment was one of many moments where I have seen God's Spirit crash in over my understanding and limits and then move wondrously. He has moved over children, even very young children. In such moments, my mind wants to understand and comprehend what is happening or why it is happening. The reality is I want to put God in a box. What I mean is, if I can understand why and what, then I can live within those confines. The reality is God continues to break those confines because, when He comes at another time, it looks different. Yet again I try to understand the why and what.

When I talk to parents and children about why and what God is doing, it changes the way I see things. What I hear from the parents and children is a hunger for more of God, a deeper love for God, a change in their hearts to want to make more room for God in their lives and to have less of their own desires. What I see is fruit. When we see God come and crash down on adults, sometimes that is easier to accept, but when God comes and crashes down on children, it is much harder to accept.

God breaks our limits and boundaries of what He is doing. Jesus did not stay away from anyone. Everyone was worthy of His time. Everyone—no matter what age, what gender, what status, what religion, what mental state, what sin state, and what political party—everyone was worthy of His time. Jesus was God in flesh on the earth, and Jesus carried the Spirit of God with Him. If this was Jesus, then this was God and His Spirit.

We need to remember that God's Spirit is a gift of:

1. Wisdom
2. Understanding
3. Counsel
4. Courage
5. Knowledge
6. Willingness to worship and serve God
7. Fear of the Lord (wonder)

And the fruit of His Spirit is:

1. Love
2. Joy
3. Peace
4. Patience
5. Kindness
6. Goodness
7. Faithfulness
8. Gentleness
9. Self-control

Many times, I have seen children experience the fruit of the Spirit in the classroom. They have also felt the gifts of the Spirit upon them. Pastor Bill Johnson often says we do not believe in a Junior Holy Spirit. He says this because we believe the size of children, their ages, their level of development, their maturity, all somehow affect the ability of God to move in, on, through, and among them. But God is no respecter of people. In Acts 10:44–46, it says,

> *While Peter was still speaking these words, the Holy Spirit fell upon all those who heard the word. And those of the circumcision who believed were astonished, as many as came with Peter, because the gift of the Holy Spirit had been poured out on the Gentiles also. For they heard them speak with tongues and magnify God.*

We need to realize that God's goal is to invite us to have a relationship with Him. With that invitation comes the Spirit, life, and promises He has for us. We *all* get to have what God wants to give us. No one is off limits, but it is our choice. Children are more willing to experience God because of their level of faith. They have less to process before they believe. Some children can simply believe, and it seems as though their level of faith is effortless. What I have come to believe is that, if it feels like God, it looks like God, and it lines up with Scripture, then it is God. Our children are walking in a level of authority and freedom simply because they have had a taste or several tastes. Children are not only walking in a level of freedom and authority, but they are also bearing fruit. When they want others to experience more of God, freedom, righteousness, and such, it has to be God.

There is so much we can learn by just creating a space for God to come. It was the moment our team decided they would not just settle for something easy. They went to God and prayed for answers on what to do next with the children. And in the simple posture of letting the children see them go to the Father for help in prayer, He came. He responded to the hunger in the room, to the call, to the posture that said, "We need You to help us." I believe He also responded to the level of faith in the room that day. It was the level of faith established by the children who knew that, when they come into this environment, they hear of what God can do, and they want it.

So many times, we have seen God come, and sometimes it is so powerful that it almost feels unbearable, and sometimes it is the tenderest and gentlest moment. At other times, it is between the two extremes. God is faithful. He wants to engage with us. Otherwise, He would not have sent His

Son Jesus to sacrifice His life for a moment. It is an eternal moment of connection with Him. With God comes Jesus and His Spirit.

I encourage you to make some space in your heart and home for God to respond. Try not to contain Him by your boundaries and understanding. Try to receive as much as you can. God wants everyone and all of them. He does not come in pieces and parts, and He does not want pieces and parts. He wants all and everything. So, my prayer is that you simply surrender your heart and mind and just receive Him. Your home, your workplace, your car, your family, your children—give each and every one to God.

ACTIVATION

1. Get a big poster board and markers.

2. Take this poster and place it somewhere central for the whole family.

3. As a family, write down the space you want God to take in your lives (home, school, dreams, hearts, friends, etc.)

4. As you see moments in your lives when God is moving in any of these areas, record them on the board, placing a date by it as well. This poster board will become watermarks in your family. Think of it as a doorway where you mark your children's and family's growth.

Chapter 4

FAILURE IS TO BE EXPECTED

Fear not, for I am with you; be not dismayed,
for I am your God. I will strengthen
you, yes, I will help you. I will uphold
you with My righteous right hand
—ISAIAH 41:10

AS A CLASS, WE WERE ASKING OUR GROUP OF CHILDREN AGES four and five what good things God had done recently in their lives. One boy started telling us about how his mom baked him some cookies and how she burned them. Nothing in his story sounded like a "good thing." It seemed that this boy simply wanted to share a story unrelated to God or His goodness. So, I asked him, "What good thing did God do in this story?"

He paused and thought for a second. Then he said, "My mom cut out the center of one cookie that was not burned and let me have that part of the cookie."

It was a sweet story, and we were able to highlight how God gave this boy a loving mother who was willing to find the best part of a disaster and make sure he got that part of it. He realized he was special and how much God loved him because of what his mother did for him. I am not sure if this little boy knew how to share the good things God does for us or testimonies of God's goodness. In the end, we walked him through the story to find the goodness of God, and we all really loved this moment.

Failure is not a negative word here. Failure is an opportunity for growth. We have a beautiful moment in life where we can remove failure as a negative and shameful word in a mindset of growth. You should be able to create a space for children who are learning to make mistakes and not identify mistakes as failures but as opportunities to grow. As children learn to walk, they become more skilled in the act if they fall. If children stopped trying to walk after they fell one or two times, then they would never be able to become skilled walkers. They would be stuck in a place of shame and fear that they would fall instead of learning the strength of their muscles and the center of gravity. I think, if we can create a new mindset of learning with the context that failure is to be expected and experienced daily, then we would probably do more and experience more growth in our lives. Can you imagine what this could do even for adults? I am not saying we need to have people fail simply for failure's sake. I am saying we need to create a safe place for people to learn from their mistakes. This will give them a healthy outlook for growth. The goal for children is not to fail, but rather the goal is for them to grow and continue to become the best version of their God-designed selves.

How can you create a healthy space for children to fail? Another way you can say this is: How can you create a healthy space for children to learn and grow?

I once went to a training session for coaches. Actually, it was a training session of coaches training coaches. One of the most valuable principles I learned from this training was how to correct children when they have made a mistake. Using a gymnastics scenario, coaches were asked, "If your child started off in a strong floor routine pose, they bolted off in a strong run, they went into a round off, their legs were bent, but then they finished with a strong landing, how would you correct them?" As the coach to coaches went around the room to hear what each one said, he discovered they all said the same thing. It went something like this: "Great start. You were very strong, you bent your legs in your round off, so you need to fix that, but your finish was perfect." It was a positive, negative, and positive feedback. The coach to coaches said actually that was how most people give feedback, and it does not help. The reason why is all the child or athlete can focus on is bent legs. The goal is to have the child visualize what he or she needs to do rather than what he or she is doing wrong. The child or athlete most likely won't fix the bent legs; instead, the child or athlete will get hung up on the legs being bent.

What did the coach to coaches advise in this case? He said to say something like this: "Great strong start. Keep that up. Straighten those legs in the round off, and that ending was perfect."

We need to train children in the way *they should go* rather than in the way *they shouldn't go*. This coaching has changed the way I parent and address an area of correction. We most likely already know in what areas of our lives we are making mistakes. We just need someone at times to tell us to correct it by telling us how.

As you read through the next chapters, think of the applicable ways you can correct mistakes by telling children how to move forward in growth. This approach creates a safe place to fail and gives insight on how to move to the next level of being able to do what it is we are teaching them.

I will give you some examples of how this can look for you. If you have children who say they can't see something or can't hear from God or they do not want to participate, then speak life into that moment. God gives us promises of what He will do when we come to Him. For example, in Matthew 7:7, Jesus said, *"Ask, and it will be given to you; seek, and you will find; knock, and it will be opened to you."* It says ask, seek, and knock, and then it says what God says He will do. God wants us to ask, He wants us to seek, and He wants us knock. God wants to respond to us. He wants to hear from us. He wants us to look for Him. He wants to engage with us. I would say something like this to children who say they cannot hear from God: "I know that God will speak to you. I am going to pray that you can hear Him. He always wants to talk to us, and He may sound different to you than you think. He could sound like a person's voice, He could sound like a thought in your head, He could sound like a picture, He could sound like a memory, and there are many more ways He speaks to us. Just wait and see what He is telling you." Then I would move on with what I was doing, but I would check back with the children from time to time, asking if God said anything to them yet. If the children still aren't hearing God, I would encourage them that I know God wants to say something to them and He will. What I am doing is speaking the truth of who God is. He speaks to us.

It is helpful for children to know our expectations are different from God's. They need to know, however, that God will speak. This can be a journey, and it can be hard, but the goal is to never give up but to keep pressing in. It took one of my daughters nine years to encounter God and hear from Him. It was a long journey for her, and a lot of what negatively impacted her ability to hear had to do with what she heard others say, how they experienced God and heard Him, and how she thought He would speak to her. I knew He would come, but I had not anticipated it would take nine years before she received her moment of breakthrough. It was a breakthrough moment for her and her walk with God, and she wanted everyone to experience the same God she encountered and was marked by this for life. It was amazing, but the wait was long and hard. My other girls had an easier time hearing God and connecting with Him. Every child is different in their journey.

I once had a mother come and talk to me about something she was concerned about with her child. She had told me that her son said he would spend time with Jesus in his free time. She said this made her very excited, but when she asked what he and Jesus did together, she was concerned by his response. This woman's son said that he watched a cartoon with Jesus when he was with Him. He explained that Jesus sat with him while he was watching the cartoon, and they laughed and enjoyed the show together. I asked the mother why this was concerning to her. She said that Jesus would not watch this cartoon, so it could not be Jesus. I then asked the mother what her son's favorite thing to do was. She responded by saying watching this cartoon. I asked how her son felt after he spent time with Jesus watching this cartoon. She said he felt full of life and joy, and he felt loved by Jesus. I told her that I didn't think that her son was wrong. I said that Jesus wants to connect with us and that is the most important goal. If watching a cartoon was her son's favorite thing to do, then of course Jesus would come and be with her son, enjoying the things he enjoyed. If her son felt as if he was full of life and joy and felt loved by Jesus, then this was fruit of the Spirit. I explained that, on the other hand, I would have been concerned if there was no fruit. Since her son was connecting to Jesus and walked away full of life, joy, and love, then from what I knew, it was more likely Jesus watching with him than any other person or spirit.

We have to make room for Jesus to break our boxes of what we think He should look like or be like. This is the Jesus we read about in the New Testament. He came in an unconventional way. He ministered to the most unlikely people. He communed and stayed with the most unliked and most undeserving. He did the most unconventional things. Most of the people did not recognize the Son of God because they had assumed He would come and He would act in certain ways. Jesus is love, Jesus is joy, Jesus is life, and Jesus is about connection and communion. Everything this mother told me about her son's "hangout time" with Jesus felt just like Jesus to me.

We have had times where other children in church did not want to believe they could hear from God or see someone healed. There was a level of fear of failing or believing in something so big that they didn't even want to try. The approach to every child in every situation will vary, but the main message is telling them who God says He is and telling them what God says He will do. His Word is full of promises, and His Word is full of promises fulfilled. We also have many stories in the Bible that lead us through a person's journey of failure, but most of those stories of failure demonstrate redemption at the end. I say "most" because the journey is two-sided. God will give us more chances if we are willing to partner with Him. If we try to do things on our own apart from Him, then there will not be life.

As a parent and as a teacher my goal is to champion the journey of children. Sometimes it feels that, if I could do part of the journey for them or take the process away, it would be easier, but that is not true. All children and adults need to have their own connection with God, but they need others to come around them and metaphorically hold up their arms until the breakthrough comes. Just like the coach to coaches said, we need to tell them what they need to do, what is possible, how things will look, and how things will be. The promise is right there in front of them. They need to walk toward the promise and get that fulfillment of the promise. We need to be the biggest fans of our children walking into the arms of their Creator and experiencing their own relationship and connection with Him.

ACTIVATION

1. Set out some paper, markers, and coloring pages, and ready some worship music.

2. Using the paper and markers, have your family write down some good things God has done for them this past week.

3. Now play some worship music, and have everyone draw their own picture or color a coloring page as a way to express thankfulness to God for the good things He has done for them.

4. Take time at the end to have each person share what they wrote down, drew, or colored.

Chapter 5

BUILDING AND EXERCISING SPIRITUAL MUSCLES

But those who wait on the Lord shall renew
their strength; they shall mount up with
wings like eagles, they shall run and not be
weary, they shall walk and not faint

—Isaiah 40:31

ONE MORNING IN OUR SUNDAY SCHOOL CLASSROOM, THE teachers came in wanting to do something concerning the prophetic with the one-year-olds. The two teachers decided to pray together and ask God what they should do. One said that they should try to find a way to have the children discover who they were by hearing from God. The other teacher decided to pull toys of two different colors and have the children choose a toy they were drawn to by its color. To make it more significant, the teachers decided to ask God which color they heard Him highlight to them about each child and then see if the child chose the same color the teachers had received.

As the teachers prayed and asked God to show them a color for each child, amazingly, both of them got the same color every time for the six children that morning. And even more surprising, each child picked the same color the teachers had selected for them. For example, when the teachers prayed for the first child, they both thought God was highlighting the color blue. Later on, the teachers took two toys, one red and the other blue, and placed them in front of the first child. Next, they looked at the child and asked, "What toy is God showing you?" The first child chose blue. And blue was the color that the teachers had selected for the child. Again, this happened every time!

Another thing that the teachers did was, before the class started, they asked God why He showed them the color He did for each child, and then they wrote down the explanation He gave them on a piece of paper for each child, later handing the papers to the respective parents of each child.

The prophetic is only one spiritual area of many in which we can intentionally train our children. In the following chapters, I am going to talk about each area that we build with our children spiritually. The goal is to hear the heart of why we do what we do with our children and then offer some practical information on how we do what we do with our children. My husband and I have used each of these areas to help our children build their own spiritual muscles. I hope you take what you want from this information and build with your own children in these areas. The same principles and practices can be applied to anyone at any age. Feel free to use this same approach for yourself as you would for a child. I may not touch on every area that a Christian would call spiritual. What I will touch on are areas that I have done with my own children and children in church for decades. What I will cover are areas that we have seen actually happen in our children.

First Corinthians 3:2 says, *"I gave you milk, not solid food, for you were not yet ready for it. Indeed, you are still not ready"* (NIV). Developmentally as infants, we naturally grow and build our physical muscles. The same thing can be said about spiritual muscles. These spiritual muscles build our connection, relationship, character, and identity in God. There is a growth and development that needs to happen. As 1 Corinthians 3:2 points out, there is a progression to growth. We do not just become strong in an area we have never experienced before. Children must learn to move their arms and legs, kicking and batting, before they can crawl. They must crawl before they can stand, and they must stand before they can walk. All of these progressions have a value and purpose in building strong muscles. The principle of development is the very same for building strong spiritual muscles. We need to build up their spiritual muscles a little bit at a time.

Have you ever built a sandcastle? In order to build a "strong" structure, you need a few elements. Sand is the most important element in building a sandcastle, but there are many elements and tools that you need to engineer the sand to its potential of becoming a strong sandcastle. You need the right wetness in the sand, or it will crumble or crack or slide away from the original structure you are molding. Once you figure out the right wetness of the sand, then you can move onto the right tools. There are buckets of different sizes and shapes, shovels, carving tools, sifters to create effects, and so much more. Now, once you have your tools and the correct wetness in your sand, you need a design concept. This design has to have a wide base and solid foundation to build upon. You could find yourself building and rebuilding to adjust the final design of your castle. All of this to say that there are a lot of steps, and the order of the steps is important to create a sound sandcastle. Without the right wetness of the sand, you cannot create the proper foundation. Without the proper tools, you cannot build the right foundation. There are many parts interlinked, all dependent upon one another to build a strong sandcastle.

Growth is an essential part of life. We need growth to build and become a better version of ourselves. There is a time of infancy, but that stage should not last too long. If we stay in this stage too long, there is a delay in development, and intervention needs to happen to help build and develop into a healthy and strong version of ourselves.

True healthy growth is always improving and moving forward. Children have a natural tendency to go farther, move quicker, and do more than they may be capable of. They show this natural tendency to do more by communicating frustration when they are not able to do what they want to do. I have been around hundreds if not thousands of babies and toddlers who are always trying to push past their natural stage of development. It is inside us to always grow. This is a principle of the Kingdom of Heaven. The Kingdom of Heaven is always *advancing*. This means that we are moving forward with a purpose in mind or to make progress. This is what we are designed to do. If we get to a place where we are not advancing, then we are becoming sedentary. Sedentary means we stop moving, and we become still in one place or seated in one place. You know what happens when we become sedentary? Our bodies register this as the stage of the beginning of death. Our bodies start to register that we are now slowly shutting down. Growth and development are vital to our lives.

Focusing on spiritual growth, which I like to call *building your spiritual muscles*, involves but is not limited to: prayer, worship, reading God's Word, prophecy, ministering to your spirit, encounters with God, and hearing God's voice. These specific areas are the areas I am going to focus on later in this book. They are easy and effective ways to help build spiritual muscles in your children at any stage of their lives. We start as early as one day old. In fact, I would speak to my babies in the womb. I would worship, read God's Word, pray over them, and speak to their identities and their spirits while they were in my womb. We can expose our children to the Kingdom of Heaven at any stage of their lives.

I had a conversation with God about the earliest stages of a child's development, and what God revealed to me has changed the way I view what is possible with children. One day, while pregnant with one of my girls, I was in awe of a baby in the womb knowing the voice of her parents. Speaking to your baby while he or she is in your womb is encouraged. Babies can hear as early as eighteen weeks gestation. Then I started to recall Psalm 139:13, *"For You formed my inward parts; You covered me in my mother's womb."* I recalled the Holy Spirit hovering over the waters in creation in Genesis and how God created Adam, forming his body from the elements of the earth. In Psalm 139:13, it talks about *knitting* in the NIV version. Then I recalled the importance of speaking to your baby while in the womb so that the baby would know your voice.

Have you ever noticed newborns, who cannot see clearly by the way, turn their heads in the direction of the voice of their mother or father when their parents speak outside of the womb? It really is a beautiful and astonishing moment. For infants to recognize the voice of their parents is a wonder in and of itself. It caused me to imagine God's hands knitting and covering every child in their mother's womb. Every child, *every child*, has had the hands of their Creator all over them while in the womb of their mother. If a child can hear the voice of their parents inside and outside of the womb, then they must know the presence of God inside and outside the womb. This discussion with God was changing the way I looked at Proverbs 22:6, *"Train up a child in the way he should go, and when he is old he will not depart from it."*

Every child comes into our natural world with a fresh nine-month encounter with their Creator. This means that a child born into an agnostic home, an atheist home, a Muslim home—any home at all—has come from an encounter with God as He formed them in their mother's womb. So just as a child would recognize their parents voice, then they are able to recognize the presence of their Creator, God of Heaven and Earth. This is why we must train children in the way they should go, and when they are old, they will not depart from it. If we don't, they can and will lose that connection with God.

They need to continually be shown how to find Him, hear Him, see Him, wait for Him. This is the most important call for parents to know—to know that we have been gifted with our children, and it is first our most important role to help our children learn to stay connected with God. We want to teach them how never to lose that connection.

Building the spiritual muscles is an important discipline to each person. We must see that we are built to grow in every area of our lives. It takes work and dedication to grow. It also will be the most valuable thing you can do to help your children to know who God is. This is also important for each of us to do for ourselves.

One thing I have learned from being a parent is children look to us as their examples. They want to know that what you teach is also what you practice. What we give them should come from the best of what we have learned from our own lives. Then this will be the foundation on which they stand. Since you have given your children a higher foundation than what you have been given from your parents or generations before you, then this next generation has a greater foundation to stand on and naturally build upon. Our goal should be for our children or this next generation to go far beyond where we have ever gone. That would be the greatest compliment and inheritance we can give to our children. The natural progression should be that multiple generations would go farther and longer than we have ever gone. This is how you pass revival from one generation to another.

1. Grab several items around your house, and place them on a table or in a bowl.

2. Have each family member take time to ask God what item He is highlighting to them on the table or in the bowl.

3. Then have each person ask God why He highlighted that item. Have them ask God whether the object is for them or for someone else.

4. Then have each person write down what God said on a piece of paper and give it to that person or keep it for themselves.

5. Make sure you have a spot to collect your words—a binder, a box, or a special place—and read them often to each other.

Chapter 6

MINISTERING TO THE CHILDREN'S SPIRITS

*Whoever has no rule over his own spirit is
like a city broken down, without walls*
—PROVERBS 25:28

OUR CHURCH HAS A STREET MINISTRY, AND ON SUNDAYS WE bring people from the streets of our city to church and feed them. We often get a grandmother who will bring her infant grandson and check him into our ministry. Our infant room writes prophetic words for each child and hands them to the parents at the door when they pick them up at the end of their time with us.

After several weeks, this grandmother said her son, the father of her grandson, was with her on one morning when she asked to make sure we wrote one of those papers for her. She said the only reason her son, the father of the baby, was there on that particular morning was because he started reading what was written on the papers. What our team was doing was releasing hope to this family. Their family was experiencing the third generation of homelessness. The father of the child was open to coming into a church building for the first time just because of what God had to say about his son. He was attracted to the hope of what God wanted for his infant boy.

One of the most incredible moments in my walk with God was when I was able to take an infant and speak identity right over the baby while I would stare deeply into the baby's eyes. Have you ever had a baby stare at you? The kind of stare where they are fixated on every part of your face? These little people are being held right in front of me all the time, and I get to tell them all about who they are and who God says they are. Not only that, I get to tell them all about Jesus and what He did on the cross for them and for us all. Then I get to tell them about the Holy Spirit and how He is here to guide and help us. If you have never done anything like this before, I recommend you try it, and you will see how it will change you. We want to show these little lives how valuable they are, and it is all because of their Creator—the One who designed them in their mother's womb.

There are many ways to attain ultimate health and wellness like exercising regularly, eating a healthy and well-balanced diet, getting enough rest, setting goals and action plans to achieve these goals, having healthy boundaries in relationships and life responsibilities, and the list can go on and on. God's Word is such a beautiful guide to lead us in the direction of health and wellness. The Bible is designed to breathe life and wholeness into us. Also, it is designed to help us remember what to do, who we are, who others are, why we do what we do, and who God is. This ultimate guide in life is always available to us. I will admit that at times it is very difficult to apply or even understand, but the goal is to always pursue and grow spiritually with God's Word and His Holy Spirit.

Just like adults, children also have spirits. That concept right there can be very obvious to some but also as complex as it is simple. We may know that we all have spirits because God's Word states that a body apart from the spirit is dead (see James 2:26). The flesh and spirit are two different parts of us. One is eternal, and one is carnal. Additionally, they cannot function apart from each other. We have a responsibility to keep our spirits healthy just as much as our bodies and minds. Just as you would put energy and time into making your body and mind healthy, you need to do the same for your spirit. The good news is you can minister to your spirit at any time. This means a mother can even minister to a baby's spirit in the womb. Developmentally, a baby hears the voices of people as early as eighteen weeks of gestational development. Arthur Burk has created some great tools for this specific time for babies in the womb.

In our classes and in our homes, we have used many great tools to minister to our children and even ourselves. The easiest way to minister to your spirit is to speak sound, identity Scriptures over yourself. You can do the same over your children to minister to their spirits. So many times, we will start our day holding babies and speaking Scriptures to them and over them. God made us spirit, soul, and body. Our spirits are most aware of the Spirit of God. God made us uniquely in His image, and His image or likeness is a trinity. It is amazing to think that we, as humans, have three parts to us as well. We are not God but designed by God to reflect Him. So like our souls and bodies, our spirits need attention and focus. Romans 8:16 states, *"The Spirit Himself bears witness with our spirit that we are children of God."* This part of us that is spirit enables us to identify that we are children of God. So, this is an important development or focus of development for all humankind.

What I think is beautiful is that it is actually very simple to speak Scripture over children and yourself. I am going to walk you through an example of how this can work. Let us look at Ephesians 2:10—*"For we are His workmanship, created in Christ Jesus for good works, which God prepared beforehand that we should walk in them."* What I would do is look at this verse and make this a declaration or a prayer, saying it aloud over a child, adult, baby, or even myself. It is a reminder of identity, helping to solidify who we are in Christ Jesus. Here is what my prayer would look like for a child named Julia:

> *Julia, did you know that you are a workmanship of God? God created you, Julia, to work with Jesus Christ who is your personal Savior. He created you to work with Him for good works. That means God wants to use your life, your words, your hands, and your relationships for good things. God knew who you were before you even existed, and His thoughts about you were with the intent to prepare you to do mighty*

and amazing things with your life. I pray, Julia, you will always know for every day you are alive that God created you to do some amazing things on this earth. Not only did He create you for amazing things, but He wanted you to be a part of the process to do amazing things with Jesus Christ as your personal Savior. Julia, may you never forget that God chose you and will always choose you because He loves you and will always love you. I pray that you will watch God use your life to show the love and power and grace of God to others. Amen.

This is such a powerful way to sow into the lives of others, especially if you are an intercessor. If speaking Scripture or praying aloud over people is hard for you to do, the Bible is full of great truths that talk about why you were made and created. The Bible is full of stories of how God can use the youngest, the smallest, the overlooked, the outcast, the most hated, and so forth. God wants us to know why we were made and for what reason. This is the simplest and easiest way to minister to each other. If you do this, you will also most likely set a standard of what others can do for themselves and those around them. How powerful this could be to a whole generation if we could give this one simple tool to our children.

Have you ever seen the videos of children speaking powerful statements to themselves in the mirror? I believe that this one approach is very effective because the children are looking at themselves in the eye in the mirror and are saying some incredible things to themselves. If you have not seen this, please do yourself a favor and google it. You will smile the whole time and may even shed some tears. I cried when I saw this because I wish someone would have done this to me or shown me how to do this for myself when I was younger. The confidence in the children who do this will skyrocket because they eventually will believe what they say about themselves. We are seeing and will see our children thrive in confidence in their God-ordained identities as we practice this simple act.

I recommend that you make sure to look at the children in their eyes as you say things over them. Eye contact is a vital part of communication. It shows that you are interested, intentionally focused on them. You are saying they are important to you. Eye contact in and of itself shows value and confidence. You are imparting something valuable to each person as you make eye contact with them. I encourage you to start by ministering to your own spirit or to a child's spirit. This is an easy place to begin in making an impact on your life or that of a child's. My husband and I do this from time to time for ourselves. My husband has also done this to his students whom he teaches in a private Christian junior high school. This is so valuable to anyone, at any age, at any stage of their lives. You could even do this over the elderly in convalescent homes. That would be an incredibly powerful ministry as well. I can see children now, ministering to the older generations in convalescent homes. Wow! What a gift we can be to each other.

I encourage you to find some great scriptural truths and implement this in your life. In the activation section, I have some powerful declarations you can use as a place to start. I also encourage you to look into Arthur Burk's resources as he has done a lot of the leg work for you. Many times, we have used his books and resources for our children's ministry, for ourselves, and for others. You can also create your own since the Bible is full of great truths meant to feed your spirit and soul.

ACTIVATION

Here are some prayers or declarations for you.

But now, thus says the Lord, who created you, O Jacob, and He who formed you, O Israel: "Fear not, for I have redeemed you; I have called you by your name; You are Mine" (Isaiah 43:1).

_____ (insert name here), the Lord created you! He formed you in your mother's womb. You are not a mistake. you were made and created for a purpose. _____ (insert name here), may you always know that God has redeemed every part of your life. Nothing will ever be wasted because God is good and He is working all things in your life for good. Even if it does not feel good now, it will be good in the end. _____ (insert name here), may you never partner with fear. Fear was paid for on the cross, and it is no longer yours to carry. God is calling your name. Pause and be silent, wait until you hear God call your name. He wants to speak to you and know everything about your life. _____ (insert name here), may you fully know and never forget that you are always His! Forever, He is yours, and you are His. Amen.

"I am the vine, you are the branches. He who abides in Me, and I in him, bears much fruit; for without Me you can do nothing" (John 15:5).

_____ (insert name here), I am God, and I am deeply rooted in you. Your identity comes from Me. I am the vine, and you are a part of Me, the branches. If you, _____ (insert name here), are the branches, then you are with Me. You are abiding in Me, and I am abiding in you. Your life, every part of you—your voice, your mind, your hands, your heart—was made to bear a whole lot of fruit. The great thing is I am a part of you, and so with Me you will do some incredible things that will influence the world around you. Remember,_____ (insert name here), I am always here with you. Without Me, you can do nothing, but with Me you can do so many amazing and wonderful things. Amen.

Chapter 7

PROPHECY

But he who prophesies speaks edification
and exhortation and comfort to men
—1 CORINTHIANS 14:3

ONE SUNDAY MORNING IN OUR FOUR-YEAR-OLD CLASS, WE had a little girl visiting us for the very first time. There is a part of our Sunday program where we carve out time for children to give prophetic words to other children in the classroom. One little guy shared something with a new girl who was visiting for the first time, a girl whom no one had ever met before. He told her, "God wants me to tell you, 'Happy Birthday,' and that your parents love and miss you a lot. They miss you so much and want to throw you a birthday party even though they can't. God loves you so much, and He is wrapping His arms around you right now."

This little girl had tears streaming down her small, red cheeks. She did not want to share or talk as the teachers and children continued to love and comfort her.

Later on, when she was picked up, one of the teachers stopped the woman assumed to be the child's mother, pulling her aside to let her know what had happened during the prophetic time. The teacher learned that this little girl was a foster child and was new to this family. The teacher also discovered the little girl's birthday was that week and all she wanted was to be with her parents on her birthday and to get hugs from them. The foster parent let us know that the little girl would not be able to be with her parents as they were in jail. Even though this little girl's life was sad at the moment, our team was so blown away at how God told her how much He loved her. The team was also able to tell the parents of the little boy who gave the word to the girl how clearly he had heard God and His heart for others.

I'm reminded of the science experiments we used to do in school. I was always intrigued and drawn to the ones with plants and water. I remember one project I chose to do. It was the one where three plants are exposed to different kinds of music. One was classical music, one was hard rock or rap, and the other plant wasn't exposed to music at all. The goal was to see how each plant responded to its musical environment and whether or not there were any observable differences in the growth or appearance of each plant. As I recall, the plant exposed to the soft classical music generally did much better than the other two plants. Knowing that environments can affect growth was very interesting to me.

I also read about a study, albeit controversial, by a man named Masaru Emoto. It was an experiment on water that was similar to the experiment with plants. Words were taped to individual jars of water. There were positive words and negative words used for the jars. The experiment looked at the molecular cells of the water before the experiment and after the experiment. The water exposed to the negative words had the molecular cells that were rigid and fractured in a way. Meanwhile, the water that was exposed to the positive words had beautiful balanced molecular cells. It was almost like what you see when you look at snowflakes under the microscope. The concept from the experiment was that the cellular level of a living organism can be affected by its environment. Here is what was extremely interesting to me about these particular experiments. The idea that words and environment, among other things, can change us from the inside out is incredible. The way God designed us and the world around us is astonishing. Our adult human bodies are made up of up to 60 percent of water. According to H. H. Mitchell, in the *Journal of Biological Chemistry 158*, the brain and heart are composed of 73 percent water, and the lungs are about 83 percent water.[1] If we are made up of a high percentage of water, what do words we think or hear do to us? If we are made up of this high percentage of water, what would our molecular cells look like under a microscope after our being exposed to negative words or positive words? There are so many studies in psychology that have to do with the condition of our health as it has been impacted by the trauma we as individuals have been exposed to. Imagine what we can do with our words and environments if we can change the things we hear and experience.

Prophecy is simply a way to speak edification which brings improvement to someone morally, spiritually, and intellectually. The goal in prophecy is to tell others who they are through the eyes of Jesus—through His lens that has covered all their sin and that recognizes who they are meant to be. Jesus sees people as they have been designed by the Creator God. When God the Father looks upon His children, He sees them as being perfect and blameless. The role of edification can be seen as changing the person even on the molecular level when living in a world that is carnal. The prophetic to a person is life-giving and is intended to build that individual up into whom he or she is intended to be by God's perfect design. No one should ever tear others down or speak anything that would even create the fractured molecules in a person.

How we view and speak to each person can change families, culture, and communities. Imagine with me people who are told who they are intended to be and not criticized for who they are presently. You are a child of the Almighty God and intended for great things. You will do and see greater things than Jesus did or saw. God chose you to show love, kindness, gentleness, courage, etc. If anything, you can go straight to God's Word and find why God created us, why God sent His Son for us, and what Jesus told and instructed His disciples to do. By using these three basic references, you will be able to speak truth and life to any person, even yourself. Jesus' life and value of life should never be wasted. Nor should God's creation, His children for whom He gave everything He had. We are desired by God, pursued by God, designed by God, and cherished by God. He wants us to do our life with Him and not apart from Him.

There are many ways that we teach prophecy, and there are different approaches to teaching on the prophetic. The basic core values of prophecy are prophecy should always build a person up, cheer a person up, and draw them nearer to God. When we build a person up, we are speaking identity to them. Because of Jesus' life sacrificed on our behalf, we are then covered in his blood. When we receive Jesus as our Lord and Savior, we are then viewed as heirs of Christ. We are sons and daughters of the Almighty God. This transformation is our new identity. Also, because of the Holy Spirit and the salvation of Jesus, we walk in the authority that Jesus gave to us through His life and the Spirit given to us as our Guide and Counselor. There are many verses that speak of our new identity in Christ. If we are speaking to those who have not yet received this new identity for themselves, then we still have an opportunity to speak into the identity of who they have the opportunity to become. No one is exempt from speaking identity or building them up.

To cheer a person up is bringing them joy. This is one of the fruits of the Spirit, so we naturally should be able to release this to someone through our lives, actions, and words. There are many ways to bring someone joy. One way is to tell them what God loves about them. So many times, I am drawn to people's smiles and to the uniqueness of individuals in what they do and how God also delights in each part of them. God actually took time to create us each individually in our mother's womb. So, if someone has freckles all over her face, for example, God chose this look for her, and it was a delight to create this unique detail about her.

To bring a person closer to God is the end goal. We want to tell people what God says to them in the Word of God. To speak to individuals about whom they uniquely are created and why you enjoy certain features about them brings joy to those individuals. How God delights in us as His children just as a mother and father would delight in their children is a beautiful thing. This should cause people to feel loved, valued, encouraged, special, known, and just so good. God wants to draw near to us, and this is such a beautiful way to encourage someone else to draw near to God.

We do not give space to prophetic words that do not speak edification, joy, or drawing people to God. Sometimes there will be moments where anyone can give a prophetic word that is discouraging, attached to fear, or causing a disconnect from the heart of God. If children give this kind of word, it can be a great opportunity to walk them through why they would feel this and redirect them to the heart of God themselves. One time, I had a child say he didn't have anything good to say to a certain person. I just encouraged him to keep asking God to show him something encouraging. God is so faithful to answer our call for help. In fact, He wants to answer us and help us. I kept encouraging the boy that this is God's heart and God would give him something. I was giving my faith to the child that the God I know and love will come and give him help and answers. Doing this can take time, but I encourage you to keep pressing into this level of faith. It is also a great teaching moment to show children what God has to say about them.

Ways to lead this time with children are varied. I will often start the time out with prayer. I start the time with prayers of what I am thankful for about God. This posture prepares the way for the Lord. Then I welcome the Holy Spirit to give us guidance and counsel. Next I ask children to ask God to show them a picture, a Scripture, a word, a song, a color, an item, or any other thing that God wants to give them for the other person. Then I say, "Once you see, hear, or think of something, let me know." If they do not get anything, then I keep encouraging them to keep asking God to show them something. If they still cannot think of something, then I will ask children to say what they see or think of when they look at the person for whom they are getting a prophetic word. Another approach would be to encourage them to draw a picture for a person. Then once they are done drawing the picture, you can ask them to ask God what it is about this picture that would be special to the person. There are limitless possibilities to how this can work.

You could have some items picked out from around the house. You could have some worship music playing in the background, and you can color pages, make things from Playdough, build something with Legos, etc. Then afterward you could ask children to create something or have them select an item from what you have gathered from around the house. You could ask them to think of someone whom God is showing them. Once they think of that person, ask them what God wants to say to them about the items or creations made during worship. Sometimes the simplest thing can be to give someone a picture and to tell that person that they created the picture during worship and God made them think of the individual. Just the idea that God put someone's name or face in another person's mind to give something so simple yet special makes people feel loved by God.

I will include some practical examples the activation section for you to try at home. Before I list these out for you, I pray that God will start to reveal more of His heart and love for you and each person on which you practice this beautiful gift of edification. You are going to bless people by doing the simplest acts of kindness, love, and joy. I pray your level of faith increases as you get to watch God speak, show, and remind you of some incredible things for others. I know that not only will the people you minister to be encouraged, but your children will also grow in their awareness of God and encouragement, and you yourselves will grow in your love and encouragement of what God is going to do with this part of your life. The world is waiting for hope, courage, joy, and the love of God! I am anticipating lives to be forever impacted and changed for the better. I cannot wait to hear all about what God is doing with the simplest acts of prophetic ministry.

ACTIVATION

1. Draw pictures and give them to someone. Go a little further and ask God to give you something special related to the drawing—something that He would want to say to the person to whom you are giving the drawing. It could be a Scripture or a simple statement like, "You are loved by God."

2. Paint some rocks with pictures, images, or words, and give them away.

3. Write down some Scripture verses.

4. Think of some people in your life and write them a card as if it were from God, and give it to them.

5. Write one phrase words of identity on a piece of paper, and tape it to an item. Then have the smaller children ask God to pick an item, and have them give it to someone. Some of the words you can write are: chosen, royal, kind, worshiper, father, mother, loyal, friend, etc.

6. Pick a color of paper. Find the meaning of the color, and write it down. Give it to someone.

Endnote

1. Water Science School, "The Water in You: Water and the Human Body," USGS: Science for a Changing World. Accessed April 2, 2021. https://www.usgs .gov/special-topic/water-science-school/science/water-you-water-and-human-body?qt-science_center _objects=0#qt-science_center_objects/.

Chapter 8

PRAYER

*Therefore I exhort first of all that supplications,
prayers, intercessions, and giving of thanks be
made for all men, for kings and all who are
in authority, that we may lead a quiet and
peaceable life in all godliness and reverence.*
—1 TIMOTHY 2:1–2

I WAS HELPING IN A THREE-YEAR-OLD SUNDAY SCHOOL CLASS-room one morning. After some playtime in the room, we gathered the children to sit at the corner of the room. We then wanted to pray over our day together, and I asked the children if one of them would volunteer to pray for our day. One little boy raised his hand. I initially thought how bold of this little boy to volunteer, especially since he was visiting us for the very first time that morning. When I brought him up in front of the other kids to lead us in prayer, he whispered in my ear, "I want to pray, but I don't know how."

"If I lead you in how to pray, would you like to repeat the prayer after me?" I whispered back in his ear.

He was very excited that I was about to help him pray. I led him through a very simple prayer of asking God, Jesus, and the Holy Spirit into our day, looking for Their leadership of us.

After the prayer, this little guy told me that he had never prayed before in his life. It moved me to tears to know that he was so bold and excited and had a desire to pray even though he didn't know how to pray or didn't even know what prayer was. I was able to tell him, "Prayer is talking to God. It is like we just say whatever we feel, need, or want to share with Him. There is also a time for us to ask God what He wants to do, how He feels, or anything He wants to share with us. So, talking to God is like talking to a friend. We tell Him everything, but then again, we are a good friend back to God. We listen and ask Him what He is doing or wants to do."

Prayer is such a perfect gift that God has given us, and we have an opportunity to teach this gift and steward it well with our children. I can remember many moments in my childhood that marked me with my parents' prayer time. Every time our family was experiencing a difficult moment, I can remember my mom or dad reaching out to their community to help cover them in prayer. My grandfather would swim laps as a workout later in life, and he would pray for each grandchild during each lap of his workout each day. Every single night before my parents would go to bed, they would spend time praying over us children and our future spouses and children before they went to sleep. A lot of my childhood memories can point to moments of my parents and grandparents setting time aside to pray over the next generations.

I am not sure that I have adopted a deep, intercessory prayer life, but I have found that my connection to God is in prayer and has been during the majority of my relationship with Him. I have spent many nights praying, and sometimes I have prayed selfish prayers. But I have always gone to God with my needs, questions, desires, and dreams. I often ask God for help and direction in decisions I have to make. As a teenager I signed up on a 24-hour prayer slot each week to take time to spend in focused prayer on things for which our church was contending. I believe that, because I had someone to model to me what a posture of prayer looked like, I found value in it. When you are shown value in something, then you are more likely to see the value and follow suit.

Modeling prayer is an area of life that we really need to build up, especially in our children, from an early age. Children need to know one way to connect with God is in the posture of prayer. The way to teach this and many of the cornerstones of Christian lifestyle core values is to model these to your children. Take time to set aside time to pray. I think we may do this at meals or bedtime, but we want our children to know that God is waiting to hear from us and He is there to listen to what is in our hearts and minds.

I find myself speaking to God throughout my day. One time in church we heard a speaker tell us that she put a timer on her phone or watch to go off every twenty minutes or so. Once this timer went off, it would be a reminder for her to pray. This was such a simple way to show how we could train ourselves to stop in our day and connect to God. My husband has done this many times in difficult seasons while he was at work. He has set his timer and has given God praise and thanksgiving, or he has stopped and waited until he felt the presence of God. It has taken a few minutes out of his day to connect his heart to the heart of God, and it has literally changed the whole environment of his day. I believe that this shifted my husband's heart to stop and give acknowledgment to God in his workday and not to try to navigate through his workday alone. I am telling you this really makes a world of difference in any environment you are in. It also trains you to stop in your day to be aware that the God who created the heavens and the earth is here right now with you, waiting to be acknowledged and invited into what is going on in your life.

There are many forms of prayer, just as there are many reasons that we may dial up a friend or a family member and give them a call. I think Christians often use prayer as a call for help. We beg God to see our situation and intervene. The reality is that God is all-knowing and He sees everything and is already there with you. Now there is a time to call on the Lord, and I do want to make sure that you hear that I am saying calling on God is valid. I'm simply saying that we don't want begging God to do something to be the only posture of our hearts in prayer.

Here are different postures of our hearts in prayer found in Scripture. In Colossians 4:2 says, *"Continue earnestly in prayer, being vigilant in it with thanksgiving,"* We must come to the Father, being vigilant in prayer with thanksgiving.

This involves keeping watch for something to come that could be dangerous. And yet, while we are being watchful, we need to make sure that thanksgiving is always on our lips. Thankfulness keeps us in a place of knowing we are aware of what God has done and is doing in our lives. It is a way of honoring God in our hearts in our relationship with Him. There is also a sense of taking the focus off ourselves in our prayer and telling God that He is doing great things.

I cannot get away from James 5:13–16, regarding prayer. It says,

> *Is anyone among you suffering? Let him pray. Is anyone cheerful? Let him sing psalms. Is anyone among you sick? Let him call for the elders of the church, and let them pray over him, anointing him with oil in the name of the Lord. And the prayer of faith will save the sick, and the Lord will raise him up. And if he has committed sins, he will be forgiven. Confess your trespasses to one another, and pray for one another, that you may be healed. The effective fervent prayer of a righteous man avails much.*

Right here, we have James's thoughts on how to come to the Father in prayer. His words are very helpful to us.

Calls for prayer, songs, prayers of faith, prayers of confession, and prayers that are done in passion are all beneficial. There are also prayers of agreement where, when two or more are gathered in Jesus' name, He is there and will grant an agreed upon request. We read about this in Matthew 18:19–20. There are also prayers of the Holy Spirit that we see in

Romans 8. Then there are prayers where we simply hand whatever is on our hearts over to the Father as Jesus did in the wilderness. Having a connection and relationship with God involves communication. We have many ways of communicating; therefore, we have many ways of praying.

Take time in your day to set up a routine to pray other than at meals or bedtime. The most significant and powerful times of prayer I have seen are when I have invited my children to pray with me in many different times and types of prayer. I have been in tears, lost to know what to do, and my children have said, "Let's pray." When my family has a dream or desire, we set time aside to pray. When others in our lives are in crisis, my children have run to their sides and immediately declared thanksgiving to their God and declared what God has done and will do again because He is good and able. When I see my children take ownership of their own personal connection with God, and when I see them walk in the authority of that relationship, it is a good day.

ACTIVATION

Here are some activations you can do together as a family in prayer:

1. Pray for a people group or nation with your family. Get out a map or globe, and gather your family together around it. You may even want to ask your children which people group or nation you are to pray for and what God wants to release to them.

2. Pray for a neighbor in your neighborhood. Spend time blessing this neighbor in their family life, health, provision, and relationship with God. Take a walk in your neighborhood together with your children, and have each of them speak a word of hope over the homes of your neighbors as you pass by them.

3. Pray over your home. Take some time to walk around your home. Pray prayers of blessings, protection, joy, love, righteousness, and salvation over each room of your home. Do this several times a year. This way anyone who comes into your home has the same prayers sowed into them.

4. Take a night to write down some notes of thankfulness, and read them aloud together.

5. Take time in worship together with your family. Spend this time picturing Jesus in front of you, and give Him all your love in worship.

6. Take communion together as a family, and take time to put the confession of sin on your lips to God. Give God all of your heart even the hardest, most unattractive parts of your life. Let God fill you up with love after you put all of the confessions on your lips.

7. Put some soft music on, and let the Holy Spirit intercede on your behalf. Imagine His words falling over you constantly like a waterfall as you rest in the presence of God.

8. Take time to pray for sick people or friends. Take a piece of paper and color markers, and write down the sickness of the person for whom you are praying. Now imagine Jesus on the cross, and remember His life was not wasted and He died for everyone to be free, even from sickness. Take this paper and put it in a bowl of water. Watch as the water washes away the sickness on the paper, and imagine this is what Jesus did on the cross.

9. Take some time to sit together as a family and read Psalm 40. Highlight each verse that tells you what God did (e.g., "You heard my cry.").

10. Take time together and write God a letter of what is on your heart and mind. Ask God questions. Take time to listen to God and hear what He has to say to you.

My prayer for you and your family is that you grow in your prayer lives and that you will see God is waiting for you and your family every time you go to Him.

Chapter 9

HEARING HIS VOICE

To him the doorkeeper opens, and the sheep
hear his voice; and he calls his own sheep by
name and leads them out. And when he brings
out his own sheep, he goes before them; and the
sheep follow him, for they know his voice
—JOHN 10:3–4

MY FRIEND WALKED INTO A ROOM OF THREE-YEAR-OLDS. As she walked into the room, a little boy pointed to her large pregnant belly and said, "Your baby died, but now is alive."

My friend's eyes welled up with tears and said, "Yes, you are right. Jesus raised my baby from death."

You see, God told this little boy this truth, and somehow this little guy heard God. He told this little guy a simple statement that was not just for this little boy to know but to remind my friend of what God had done. Let me explain.

Several months before, my friend woke up in the night to severe bleeding. Her fears were coming into reality. Her body was miscarrying her little child. She sat in the bathroom on the phone with her midwife, who was verifying that she was experiencing a miscarriage. My friend started to pray to God to protect the precious baby's life. At that moment, her husband walked into the bathroom, and as she looked up at him, she saw he was wearing a shirt with a lion on it. She felt that it represented Jesus Christ, the Lion of the tribe of Judah. To her, it was as if Jesus were standing in front of her. Jesus is the One who conquered death and sin on the cross. So, she declared this over her baby, "He shall live and not die."

The next day, she went in for an ultrasound and witnessed that the baby didn't have a heart rate. She kept the promise she had received in the night and kept declaring life. A few days after that, they found the baby had grown larger and had a heartbeat. Jesus raised this baby from death. To this day, her baby is alive and well.

"Hearing His Voice" is somewhat of a loaded title. I will walk you through the different ways we teach children to hear God. Most of what we teach is just from what we read and know from Scripture.

From Genesis to Revelation, there are many stories and accounts of men and women who had conversations with God. From Adam and Eve to Moses, Joseph, Samuel, Jesus, John, Peter, and many others, we see God speaks. Speaking is revelation, life, and creation. God's speaking stops the works of the enemy and much more. In Isaiah 30:21, we find that God in His mercy and grace is willing to direct the steps of a corrupt nation if they are willing to have faith and live righteously. God will tell us which way to go, how to respond, and where to look, and He will bring the right people to us if we wait and have faith, knowing that He will come with answers.

We often find that doing things ourselves is easier or quicker. Possibly in the moment, it can be. And let's face it, we like instant gratification as a culture. Imagine if we can teach our children to stop and ask for help, direction, answers, and even clarity. God is so faithful and extends to us His grace and mercy even in the most corrupt nations among great wickedness.

In the Gospel of John, we learn quite a bit about God and how He speaks to us. We learn about being God's "sheep," who hear His voice and follow Him. Jesus tells us more about God and how to connect to Him and hear Him. We also learn about the role of the Spirit of God who was given to us as a gift after Jesus left this earth. The Holy Spirit is the Spirit of God who will guide us, reveal to us, and counsel us. We learn in John 14:26 that the Holy Spirit will also bring to our remembrance the things that Jesus taught us about God or this earth and the life we are to live. We know that God is speaking to us, and He can speak through Scripture, visions and dreams, images, words, memories, wisdom, truth, His felt presence, revelation, others, and nature. He speaks to young and old alike.

If you can recall the story of Samuel in the house of Eli, the boy Samuel was dedicated to the Lord for his whole life because he was a promise from God to Hannah his mother (see 1 Sam. 3). When Samuel first came to the house of the

Lord, he did not know God yet because God had not been revealed to him. Also, it was rare in those times for God to speak or give visions. Yet God called to Samuel. This is such an amazing thought to me. God can be speaking to someone while that person may not even know Him as Lord and Savior. The most amazing reality is Jesus' life was sacrificed for our eternal connection to God. He died for all humanity that we might have a personal relationship with God. Since Jesus laid down His life so that we could relate to the God, how much more should we be able to see, hear, and find God.

We should be able to teach our children to ask God for wisdom and revelation, knowing He speaks in many different forms. God created us with different senses, and so He speaks in different ways. To limit God, then, is not in our best interest. We need to be aware that God can use, will use, and has used all kinds of things to speak to us. Remember the donkey, the bush, and the fig tree in the Bible? God used these types of things to speak, and He can use anything to get our attention and speak to us.

We want to have children who, from the very beginning in their growth and development, understand that God is speaking to them and us all. We want them to know how God speaks to us, and having them access this gift is the goal. I have four children. Each of them is very different and unique. If you have more than one child, you know that each one is very different. Even if you did not have your own children, you may have noticed differences among your siblings. You probably are very different from each other. As I've mentioned before, siblings from the same parents can be different even though they share the same genes and come from the same gene pool. This is true as well in how we all interact and hear from God very differently. For children to know this early on is really important and helpful.

We have often been known to follow by example so that in essence means what we hear and are told we will build our realities on. So, if children hear that their parents or siblings or other children hear from God in a certain way, then they themselves will begin to understand that this is how they can hear from God. Many children I have worked with have to break this comparison of themselves to others, however. We actually have to do this on a daily basis as adults. We compare our experience to that of others, and this may cause us to feel successful or unsuccessful, adequate or inadequate. Hearing how others hear from God should be like facets on a diamond. How others hear from God demonstrates part of how God speaks, but it is not the entirety of how He speaks. To know there are many more ways of communication is actually freeing and overwhelming at the same time.

To start teaching your children about hearing God speak to them, first ask them if they have ever heard God speak. Most likely, you will hear *no* as their answer. This is because we are basing how we communicate by hearing words. This is a beautiful time to talk about how we also learn what is going on and what is being said without words. We can discover what body language, as an example, can communicate. Hugging, smiling, frowning, how someone holds their head, how they walk, and how their hands and arms are placed on their body are all examples of body language. And then in verbal communication, something can be communicated in the tone or the inflection of an individual's voice. We can also receive communication through written words, through someone doing something for us, etc. Communication is not just hearing words—that's the point we want to stress with children.

We can then move on to addressing how God speaks to us in dreams, in our feelings, in music, or in His Word. Sometimes things jump out at us. People will say things to you that you were just thinking about. We like to call some of these things *coincidences*. We might think of someone suddenly and feel that the person may need prayer. We may get pictures, numbers, or colors that come to the forefront of our minds. Some people may think the random thoughts in our heads are just that, random. Yet God is very creative in how He speaks to us.

So many times, I think about someone, knowing that means to reach out to them and let them know that I am thinking about them. I then take the opportunity to ask them if I can pray for them in any way. Almost every time I do this, something is happening in that person's life at that very moment. God moves all over this planet, and He is the Creator of the whole universe. It should not be that impossible to think that He is able to put a thought into your mind that leads to a person feeling loved, known, and valued. This is the very nature of God. He is for us, and He is with us. Nothing is impossible with Him.

ACTIVATION

Here are some ways to practice listening to God with your children:

1. Ask your children to ask God for a person's name. When they think of a name, then have your child ask God what we are supposed to do for that person. If it is someone you know, take a risk, and do what God says. If it is someone you don't know, keep a notebook or note app in your phone and list the name and the thing you're supposed to do for that one. Challenge yourself to be bold to find this person in daily life.

2. Think of your favorite color. Then ask your children to ask God for the answer to your favorite color. This is not a get it right practice, although that is a goal. The purpose is to practice listening to God. Maybe they will think of a color, or maybe it will be the first color they see in their surroundings. The idea is to always ask God to help you with the answer. You can do this with animals, numbers, items, etc.

3. Ask your children about a "good dream" they had. Then have your children ask God what

the dream means. Maybe challenge yourself as the adult to ask God to help you with what the dream means. You can also find some meanings to things by searching online. For example, let's say there was a really big mountain in your dream. Search for "mountains in the Bible," and read what comes up.

4. Take the day to ask God what you should do with your day. You can offer Him an hour or two of your day or challenge yourself and offer Him most of your day. Start off by asking God what your family should do with the day? What should you make for breakfast, what park should you go to today, etc.? These are fun and easy ways to invite God into your day and life, and wait to hear what He wants to do or say.

5. Take a problem in your life that you keep having. Ask God for help and an answer on what you should do with that problem. Let's say it's as simple as losing your keys or more complex as making new friends. Take time to invite God into this part of your life, and have Him give you some answers.

6. Ask God to show you what you should draw or paint. Then ask God what colors you should use. Now ask God why He wanted you to use those colors. Write down on the back of your drawing or painting what He said to you through each question and process of your art time.

7. Take some time to read the Bible. Ask God which Scripture He wants you to read. Pray over that Scripture before you read it, and ask God to show you something for you, your family, friend, or neighbor about this Scripture. Take some time to journal it.

The goal here is to have fun, invite God into your daily life, and let Him speak through words, pictures, Scripture, songs, colors, people, memories, feelings, and much more. He is speaking and wants to speak to you. My prayer is that you hear God like you have never heard Him before—that His voice would be the loudest voice in your life—and that you would feel Him and would feel known, valued, and loved by Him. I pray your children would run to their Heavenly Father first every moment of their day and that God would move mightily over your homes and lives.

Chapter 10

ENCOUNTERING GOD

*And I will pray the Father, and He will give
you another Helper, that He may abide with
you forever—the Spirit of truth, whom the
world cannot receive, because it neither sees
Him nor knows Him; but you know Him,
for He dwells with you and will be in you.*

—JOHN 14:16–17

WE HAVE A CHILDREN'S CAMP EVERY YEAR, FOR NINE- TO
twelve-year-olds, where we go up into the mountains about
an hour away from town and go after God. We have a lot of
fun! We take children from all over the world, and we make a
space for them to worship God and hear God. We teach them
about God, have them encounter God, and let them minister
to each other with God.

One night after we spent time in worship at camp, my
friend's son had a vision from God about his little sister. In
this boy's vision, he was spending time playing with his sister.

The place was in Heaven, and this boy's little sister had passed away on Earth a few years before this vision. In the vision, his sister was running, playing, laughing, and showing her brother her life. After a while, this little boy woke up from this vision, and he felt so happy that God was showing him his sister and that she was in Heaven with a new body. She was free, laughing and enjoying herself. You see, this little boy's sister was born with severe brain damage. She had to be fed by tubes, could not move freely on her own, and could not speak. She was so incredibly beautiful, oh was she beautiful, and full of spice, so much so her hair was spicy red. It was the best kind of spice you could ever give and have in a person, too. So, this boy grew up with his sister for a short few years before she went to Heaven. He kept growing and having a life while her life here was over. Then God showed up to this little boy in the vision of his sister and her life in Heaven. This moved this boy's heart to see how full her life was with the Lord, and it started to heal his heart from the loss of his sister. This boy encountered a part of God and God's heart that was aimed directly toward him and his heart. God knew the boy's heart was hurt and broken, and God wanted to start the process to heal the boy's heart. The amazing thing is this boy had this happen a few times each time he came to our camp. It was a secret and sacred space for him and God.

The word *encounter* means an unexpected experience or meeting with someone or something. A spiritual encounter is when God crashes into your time, space, day, or heart and does something incredible. To encounter God can happen in a moment or during a lifetime. It can look the same each time or different each time. What I know is that God wants to encounter us all the time. I love that the meaning starts with an unexpected experience with someone. Part of God's nature and character is unexpected; it's a mystery and indescribable. He is unexpected in experience, but we can always expect Him to come. The mystery of God is fun, frustrating, confusing, adventurous, and so much more. It is like depths to us that we will never fully find and discover no matter how hard we try. There is so much to who He is and what He can do because He is eternal, with no ending. To explain this part of God to children, let alone adults, is very difficult. By nature, we are curious, wanting to know, discover, concur, and understand. We want to define all of God away. So, to open up Pandora's box of God's nature can be exciting but frustrating, too. I have had to become more and more comfortable in saying, "I don't know." "I don't know" eventually can be the most freeing thing you can learn to say. Why? Because we may never know. However, we can know the One who knows everything and all things, and we can trust Him.

How we teach children to encounter God in one way is to set up a space that makes room for God. We create a space full of worship because it is the posture of our hearts toward Him. Then we may wait to see what He wants to do. The spiritually hungry usually access an encounter with God easily. Also, children tend to be more willing and trusting to find God if you create the space for them to do so. They want to find Him and see Him. They want more of Him. There is less in them to process regarding how to get to Him. They just wait or ask God to come. God is faithful to show up, especially to the hungry.

Many times, you can hear people say, "More God, more," or "Fire of God fall down on us," or "God, I love You," while they wait. What they are doing is giving God their heart, time, and energy. Sometimes He comes with a crash—His presence heavy and full of force—and sometimes He just makes you feel safe or loved. There is no formula; there is no right or wrong way. He has also come into a room, and people have been offended. This is not God offending them, but their own human nature being offended that His coming or His presence doesn't look like or feel like what they expected.

If you create a space and wait on the Lord, fully pressing into the moment, He comes. It is really powerful when you have a group of people creating this space. It is Matthew 18:20—*"For where two or three are gathered together in My name, I am there in the midst of them."* God is faithful, and He wants to encounter us.

Another activation we do to encounter God with our children is we create a room with different focal points with which to interact. These focal points are stations within the room. We have created many different stations within a room that make a tangible connection with a biblical truth. The goal is to help children see what God could be saying through different Scriptures. We have also done focal points with adults for years, and they are really powerful. The stations are meant to enable adults or children to walk and engage with a clearer reality of what God is saying to them. The connection is unique to each person as well. It is like God's living Word. As we engage with God's living Word, the Spirit of God moves over it. Later I will explain what some of these can look like using specific examples from the Scriptures.

It is a challenge to create a space that encourages others to meditate upon God's Word, but the Holy Spirit gives creative ways to build the space. Just like the worship that we have done with the children at camp, the focal points provide space for God to come, and we meet Him with expectation that He will do something in this. It really is dwelling with God or even abiding with Him. As we mediate on Scripture and truth, and press into knowing more of what God wants to say about this over our lives, we are softening our hearts for God to invade and reveal a deeper understanding of who He is and who we are in Him. He never disappoints. God makes things beautiful, even if there is a process to get to the beauty. God does not waste an opportunity to invade our lives and hearts. It is imperative that we make sure that, when we create this space, we have God in mind.

You can do examples of interactive encounter moments with all ages. We have done this with the very youngest, ages newborn to twelve months, and the adults, and we have found the stations to be very effective. It is amazing how simple an act of connection and activation to invite God and see Him move over every age can be. With our youngest age groups, we use toys, blankets, music, most anything age appropriate. We also make sure that this time is fun and inviting, making our faces animated and our expressions big and exciting.

To give you an example, we had a baby blanket with the words, "Jesus loves you," on it. We took each baby individually and placed the baby on the blanket and prayed over him or her. We spoke Jesus' love over the little one and what we heard God saying, like why He loved the baby specifically. After the children had their individual moments on the blanket, to sit in the truth, we entered a time of worship with God. Doing an activity like this can be a very simple act, bringing in simple biblical truth to make this activity a foundational building block to a connection with God. Get creative with Scripture and the items you have around you. Look for certain colors, shapes, scenes, books, toys, anything that connects to God and biblical truths in His Word.

ACTIVATION

Here are a few examples of what you can do for focal points or stations. Get creative. Ask others for their thoughts and ideas, and grow this concept with interactive connection with God.

1. To make a focal point station on creation for younger children, I recommend using toys to show or create the sky, some clouds, some mountains, some trees, some animals, and some people. Set them up around the room for little children to see. Tell the children how God created each thing you have represented, and now tell the children that God created them. He chose their little nose, the color of their eyes, all their toes and fingers, the little personality they were to be. Speak over the children the different things God chose about them when He knit them together in their mother's womb. Speak about the name that their parents gave them just like Adam chose for each animal.

2. To make a focal point station on creation for older children, play some soft music in the background. Have modeling clay or molding dough. The goal is to have the children create something with it. First have them think about

what God was thinking about when He made each of us and every living thing. Then give the children a piece of paper and have them write down the things they thought were important to making a person and why. For example, if they thought pizza would be this person's favorite food, then the person they create should have a nose to smell that pizza. Have them create the nose. If the person, they are thinking about were a great skateboarder, then they should be good at balancing, so maybe the person needs some muscles. Once they finish what they would create in a person, have them try to mold this person with the dough. You could have them ask God what are some things that He chose to create specifically in them. Then have them write down God's thoughts about them.

3.   To make a focal station on love for younger children, get a big piece of fabric. Cut it into the shape of a heart. Make sure this cut cloth is big enough to wrap around the child. Lay the heart on the floor, and have the child sit in the middle of it. Now wrap the cloth around the child, and say, *"Whoever lives in love lives in God, and God in them"* (1 John 4:16 NIV).

4.   To make a focal station on love for older children, make a paper heart and have two handheld mirrors. The paper heart represents the love of God. Now, write the word, "God,"

on one of the handheld mirrors. The other mirror is just a reflection of the first mirror with the "God" on it. Have the children hold the paper heart near their faces or near their hearts. Then have the children look at the mirror with the word, "God," on it. Place the mirror behind them, showing the reflection of them looking at themselves in the first mirror with "God" on it. Now say over the child, *"Whoever lives in love lives in God, and God in them."*

Chapter 11

Worship

Let the word of Christ dwell in you richly in all wisdom, teaching and admonishing one another in psalms and hymns and spiritual songs, singing with grace in your hearts to the Lord. And whatever you do in word or deed, do all in the name of the Lord Jesus, giving thanks to God the Father through Him.
—Colossians 3:16–17

My husband and I were teaching a "parent and me" worship class of two- and three-year-olds and their parents. The class was developed to walk children into worship alongside their parents. We were doing this class for an entire week.

The first day, we saw a father come into the classroom with his little girl. The father had a walking boot that served as a cast on his leg. During the introduction of the class, we asked the father what had happened to him and what was wrong with his leg. He had mentioned that, the weekend before, he was playing at the beach with his family. As he was running around, something in his leg popped. He could not walk after that. And so, he went to the doctors. They told him that his Achilles' tendon had ruptured.

It sounded to us like he was robbed of a connection time with his family. We simply had the little children ages two and three gather around the father and pray for his leg to be healed. Then we played a song and worshiped God together by jumping up and down and running around the room singing our worship song.

A few minutes later, I looked over to see the father with the walking boot cast, and he had taken it off. In fact, he threw it across the room. He was jumping up and down and running around the room. God had just healed his leg, and the whole group kept worshiping God and running around, jumping and singing with joy of who God is and what He had done. It was truly that simple. It was miraculous!

Worshiping God is recognizing Him and giving Him your honor, affection, and attention. We don't worship Him only with songs and music; worship is a lifestyle. Worshiping God with all of our being is a daily lifestyle that changes the way we live. It is the posture of a heart that is releasing a fragrance to God. We should release words, actions, affection or emotion, and attention throughout our day to God. We want to give Him words from our lips, fruit from our lives, and thoughts in our head. We want our worship of Him to affect how we see and treat each other. The devotion of our lives is to set our gaze on God. We focus on God with deep respect and honor with our whole being.

We can worship God in Spirit and truth. Worship is a choice, and it is something that we get to do here on Earth that we will also do in Heaven. Is that not the most incredible thought, that we will worship our King on Earth and in Heaven? Another spectacular thought is that the whole earth worships the Lord. This includes the rocks, mountains, trees, and every living thing. Heaven is filled with worship, and this will be our permanent posture in Heaven. On Earth, we have a choice, so we want to choose to worship God with our lives, words, hearts, and actions. And this is such a privilege to teach our children.

To help your children enter into a life of worship means you must model it for them. Your life must show your children that worship is a priority and honor. It is a choice whereby you place value on it and give time for it. Worship should not be just in secret, especially to your children. From the moment you wake up to the moment you lay your head down, you should be living a life of worship to God, your Heavenly Father, whether it be with the words on your lips, thoughts in your mind and heart, or your focus. Worship God with music, prayer, devotion, and more. Again, this is modeled and taught by parents. I have talked a lot about how we can model this, but teaching it is as simple as explaining why we worship God to having your children lead a time of worship in your home, your car, or even on a walk.

How we can practically worship God in our families can be simple to the most creative parents. Simply teach your children to acknowledge the Lord in the morning when they wake up. I will often wake up and tell the Lord, "Good morning."

This helps me to start my day with my heart focused on Him. I will also start a conversation with God about what I am doing and how I am anticipating Him throughout my day. Worship music is almost always playing on our devices in the morning as we roam throughout the house to get our day started. From getting our breakfast to reading our Bibles, packing our lunches, and getting ourselves ready to walk out the door, we are worshiping. I play worship in my car as I drive. Our children attend a Christian private school, so they have time each day to enter into a time of worship in school. They carve out time to adore the Lord. This can be done via reading Scriptures and writing about what God is speaking to them about those Scriptures. They also have drawn pictures, worshiped with cloths, worshiped with dance, and gone through the heart of the Father through the alphabet. The heart of the Father through the alphabet can be A—God, You are Awesome; B—God, You are Beautiful; C—God, You are Caring; D—God, You are Dazzling; and others words that begin with the remaining letters of the alphabet—all the way through Z. The goal is to tell God who you see Him to be through adoring the characteristics of His heart.

Worship in dance was and is a wonderful experience for our family. Dancing was the preferred manner of worship with our four girls in our home. Along with dancing, our girls would often look through all of their clothes and toys and find dresses, outfits, and clothes to worship along with. We would play worship music that the girls were familiar with. This most likely would be the songs we sing in church. We would clear a space in a room in our home, and as a family we would worship together. Sometimes the girls would get paper and different crayons and markers, and they would draw pictures or create art while worship music was playing in the background. They would draw what they saw or felt, and it would be a gift to the Lord.

Another familiar form of worship in our home would be using music to soak or sit and rest in. Soaking provides a softer, slower worship environment. It uses soft music that may tend to be more instrumental. The environment for this approach in worship may even include softer lighting. The goal is to lay down or slow your body down and rest in worship with God. This works well at the end of the day with children before they go to bed. We would play worship music and rest in the presence of God. To wait and rest in the Lord is refreshing, relaxing, and calming. Sometimes we need to go sit with God and focus on His face or feel what He is doing in the moment. This posture of worship can help children enter into a time of sleep while spending time with the Lord. We commonly would do this if our children were dealing with a lot of fear, anxiety, or worry. It would help them feel that we were ushering in the presence of God into their rooms while they prepared to sleep. Knowing that the last thing they did before bed was to spend time with God was really helpful toward their managing the negative emotions with which children battle.

Children have a tendency to focus for one minute for each year of age they are. If they were four years old, then they could focus on one thing for around four minutes. This is a general guideline for those working with children. If there are times when children can worship God for more than the basic age development guideline, then it can be a marker for knowing that God's presence came and the children really did have an encounter with God in worship. For example, we have had times when the presence of God came into a time of worship with two-year-olds, and they soaked in the presence for ten to fifteen minutes. That truly is remarkable knowing that they should only be able to focus for around two to three minutes, yet they were able to focus in worship for five times longer than expected.

ACTIVATION

Here are some ways you can set up your home or rooms for worship for your children.

1. Make sure to have some worship music selected. My suggestion is to use worship music you are familiar with. Include music with words among the selections, as well as instrumental music. It can vary from house worship music (what you sing in your church services) to children's worship music. Worship music is available for free on many different platforms. We play it from our television.

2. Have some worship cloths available for your children. The lighter the material, the better. For younger children, it is helpful to hold onto an edge of the fabric. Tie the edge of the fabric to a hair tie or something round to place that end around the wrist of a child. For older children, a dowel can be used so the fabric can act like a flag, or they can simply hold onto the fabric themselves. Two- to three-feet squares work well for children of any age. Here is a list of fabric types that work:

   ▪ Chiffon

- Georgette
- Crepe
- Cotton Voile
- Organdy
- Silk
- Cotton Lawn
- Handkerchief Linen
- Dotted Swiss
- Batiste
- Tulle

3. Get some art paper, pens, pencils, crayons, watercolor paint, etc. Have some worship music playing in the background and have the children draw pictures of God, what God is doing, what God is saying, how they feel in worship—anything that would connect them to God and His heart.

4. Have your children dance without a worship cloth by using their body to express worship instead. They may have hand motions they might make up. They may know how to dance in different forms like ballet, hip-hop, modern, etc.

5. Have your children worship with some simple instruments. You may have egg shakers, drumsticks, a keyboard, or a triangle.

6. Have your children journal or write poems to God if they are able. David is really the perfect

worshiper represented in the Bible. He wrote so many psalms, and they are beautiful forms of worship. A lot of our worship songs come from David and his words.

I hope that you find more creative ways to enter into worship with your children. My prayer is that our families will become known for this powerful posture of worship. My desire is that we realize the full access we have to the King of all kings and that our hearts go before Him, laying aside our worries and frustrations and giving Him our full attention and complete affection. May a beautiful fragrance come from our hearts to His. May our children know that they can go to the Father freely at every point of their day, giving Him their offerings of praise.

Chapter 12

LOVE FOR GOD'S WORD

Finally, brethren, whatever things are true,
whatever things are noble, whatever things are
just, whatever things are pure, whatever things
are lovely, whatever things are of good report,
if there is any virtue and if there is anything
praiseworthy—meditate on these things.
—PHILIPPIANS 4:8

EVERY YEAR, WE GRADUATE OUR CHILDREN IN OUR CHURCH from one age group or grade group to the next. When we hit some specific age or grade groups, we celebrate their graduation with a certificate and an age-appropriate Bible. The goal is that this Bible will grow with them until they get to the next age or grade group of graduates, after which they receive their next Bible. Having our children know and connect to God's Word in each and every stage of life is a value of ours for our children. We want them to grow spiritually as they are growing physically, mentally, and emotionally.

The Bible used for the beginning stages contains a lot more pictures and very simple words and sentences than the ones used for older children. After the children learn how to read, we give them an early reading Bible. Then they may come to a point where they need to employ a certain learning style, and we have a few options to help them in this next level to learn creatively with either coloring Bibles or action Bibles. These Bibles help them connect and relate to God's Word. After this stage, they will get more of an adult Bible. Having something that is solely theirs—that they can mark, color, underline, and make notes in—is showing our children they are important and should have their own Bibles. I think it is important to share with children that many people do not even have their own Bibles and emphasize how special it is for them to have their own. We put their individual names in their individual Bibles, making it a special occasion for them to receive a Bible for themselves.

Again, like anything else we do, we are creating a "new normal" for our families. Maybe it may not be so new for you. For some, setting these values into their everyday lives at home with their children is a completely new journey, however. We do not want to create rituals out of a religious spirit, but we want to use our creativity to create ways for our children to know God and to help others know and experience God more. This needs to flow out from the heart. We develop a love and honor for God in our lives, and we can express our hearts to God in so many ways.

If trying to encourage a love and value for God's Word seems too much like a ritual, we can change that. We can help make reading God's Word not feel like just another thing we have to do by how we prepare ourselves for our time with God. The goal for this value for God's Word is to know Him more. We want to hide His Word in our hearts so that we can continue to grow. We have to develop ourselves, and developing causes us to grow and stretch, and that often looks like disciplining our time.

With children, we want to approach loving the Word of God with value and fun. God is fun, and I think that many people do not know the part of the Father who created joy! The joy of the Lord is our strength, and we need to make more space for joy in our lives. Experiencing joy with the Father will strengthen us in our desire to know God's Word. Children learn so much more when they are enjoying the process. However, I do want to make sure that sometimes we need to teach our children to press into moments of discipline, even when we are not having the best time. We should be honest with them. We all have times when we have to push ourselves during difficult days or moments of life. We have had to make ourselves do things we really did not have motivation to do. I have done this with things like working out or reading God's Word. I had to choose to do the very act of discipline, knowing that I really did not want to do it but knew that I would not regret doing it once I did. Reading His Word does bring life and value, so actually not doing it is harmful to our spiritual lives.

I have mentioned how giving your child a Bible that is age appropriate is valuable. You can research many different types of Bibles that are available today. From digital Bibles to audio Bibles and workbooks, you have many options. You know your children the best, and so I would start with what your children are drawn to naturally. Are they readers? Do they like pictures and learn better when pictures are on pages? Could they benefit from listening to an audio Bible? How about an interactive Bible?

The first step toward making reading the Bible or interacting with God's Word a part of your children's daily lives is by getting your children's hands and eyes on some form of a Bible. Then set up a schedule that works for you. Please do not start off with a big goal that you will fail in the first few weeks. I would set attainable goals. For example, maybe three to five nights out of the week you read your Bibles together before bedtime. If that goal is not realistic or it's too simple for you, come up with something more fitting for your life and family. Having a time where you all agree it is possible to meet is a great start. Letting your children speak into the schedule on what they think they may or may not be able to do will also show value to your children. Ask them when you all should read the Bible together and how long should you should read the Bible each time. You may also want to talk about what would be the easiest way to remember to read the Bible each day. Sometimes their answers may not work, but letting them have a voice in the discussion is great. They just don't need to have the final vote on how the reading time is executed. This is a team effort. The goal would be to do this together as parent(s) and children. Remember that modeling the love and value for God's Word needs to come from you.

Make reading the Bible a part of your life. You are the adult modeling reading God's Word and helping the children have an attainable goal and plan to read their Bibles. Doing this together will bring connection and conversation and is an effective way to build relationships with your children. Establishing goals with rewards is a wonderful way to build encouragement toward completing a goal. This makes attaining the goal a possibility even during moments when accomplishing the desired goal is hard. I personally do not think rewards are wrong in the Kingdom. As long as you are working toward a connection with God, He is faithful.

The apostle Paul said, *"I press toward the goal for the prize of the upward call of God in Christ Jesus"* (Phil. 3:14). The key to success in reading your Bible is movement forward or momentum. It is getting yourself familiar with the living Word of God and exposing your children to the history of God, the heart of God, the truth of God's Word, and the life instructions of His Word. Many people talk about how you can separate lies from truth, and it is by making sure you are exposing yourself to truth. If you expose yourself to truth *and* lies, then it can become difficult to distinguish between the two.

The enemy doesn't simply speak lies, but he speaks half-truths. He is the deceiver, and the deceiver must cause you to believe that what he is telling you is true so that you start to believe it *is* the truth. In order to distinguish truth from near truth, you must really know the truth. My daughter is studying for her driver's license. The questions she is practicing with have answers that are obviously wrong, but then they have answers that are partially correct. Unless my daughter studies and knows the right answer and truth, then she will be unable to select the correct answer from among those provided. She needs to truly know the material from the driver's manual, or she will be vulnerable to selecting the wrong answer. Knowing the manual is crucial to her passing the driver's written text, just like knowing God's Word is crucial to our not being deceived by the enemy's partial truths. The reality is, however, we can never know the Word through and through. But we can maintain a posture of reading the Word and learning about the living truth in the Word. The Word is alive! This means it is always revealing more and more of God. We will never master the Word because the Master Creator is always revealing more and more. There is no end to the knowledge and awareness of God. We must make sure we are willing to press into knowing and learning more about God and His Word for the rest of our lives. This is how we press on. We press on even into eternity.

The approach to a life aimed toward knowing and having a relationship with God does involve disciplines. We must keep our minds, bodies, hearts, and souls always growing and healthy. In order to keep growing and being healthy, we have to make decisions that help maintain growth and health. The good news is we do get to choose, and God is so loving that He wants us to feel powerful enough to choose. When we have power of choice, we have power over the consequences of our choices. Consequences can be either positive or negative. It is great to set the example and expectation with your children to always try to grow and improve—to try to make good choices. Please hear me when I say "try." This means there is room for growth when we do not always have the best follow through for each day. We do get to start again the next day, but as God has told us in His Word, perseverance builds character. We are becoming great people with great character when we push ourselves to keep going even after we fail. Remember my analogy of children learning to walk? If children stopped trying after they stumbled or fell the first time, second time, or even the one-thousandth time, they would never become children who master walking. This is a process, and we must make this fun and invite our children into the journey of this process.

We are not just modeling a journey to love God's Word; we are also building incredible people who get to see firsthand how to handle life when they do not see perfect results. We do not want to teach children to be perfect. We want to teach children to be the best version of themselves, and in that journey, they get to see their strengths and their weaknesses.

ACTIVATION

I am going to give some easy examples of how you can build a love for the Bible. Please know there are always other creative ways to build this love and connection. Asking others how they do this in their home is always a great resource, too.

1. Watch an age-appropriate movie about the Bible. There are some incredible biblical stories that are animated as well. Start the week by reading the Bible story in the children's Bible, and finish your week with a family movie night to watch this story. Talk about what your children liked in the movie. Ask if your children noticed any differences between the Bible story and the movie Bible story.

2. Get some coloring pages of memory verses and have your whole family try to remember a verse together for the week or month. When you have mastered the Bible memory verse, track it in some way so you all can see your progress throughout the year.

3. Create a song to help you memorize a Bible verse together. Our digital devices have some simple ways you can record your own song. Creatively

make a song using a memory verse together as a family. Make this a monthly challenge.

4. Write out a memory verse for the week or month, and have your family write down how the verse makes them feel or what this memory verse means to them.

5. Set aside time each day to read your Bible together. Take turns reading a verse or a couple of verses. Then talk about what you read and what you feel God is saying.

6. Find a Bible that you feel free to decorate its pages with coloring pencils. If the verse is about mountains, draw mountains. If the verse is about water springing out, draw water springing out. Just be creative.

7. Get some sticky notes and write one word on a sticky note for each word of the memory verse you are memorizing. Put this verse on the mirror in your bathroom, and read it while you get ready in the morning and when you get ready for bed at night. Do this for a week.

8. Write a word for each word of the verse on a piece of paper. Hide the papers around the house, and then go on a scavenger hunt. Once you find all the papers, try and put the verse together in the right order.

9. Make body movements to each word of the verse. I did this one in junior high when we memorized

Proverbs 18:10. I still remember this verse today: *"The name of the Lord is a strong tower; the righteous run to it and are safe."* Point your finger to the sky for, "The name of the Lord is." Make muscle arms for "a strong." Make your hands touch above your head, making a point with palms touching each other for "tower." Make a fist up in the air for "righteous." Run in place for "run into it." Make the baseball umpire arm cross sign for "and are safe." This will be a fun way to memorize some Scripture.

10. Write out the memory verse on a piece of paper, and have each person draw a picture that explains the memory verse. For example, Psalm 121:5–6 says, *"The Lord is your keeper; the Lord is your shade at your right hand. The sun shall not strike you by day, nor the moon by night."* Draw or paint a picture of these two verses. I bet they would look similar yet have some differences.

Chapter 13

HEALING

And as you go, preach, saying, "The kingdom of heaven is at hand." Heal the sick, cleanse the lepers, raise the dead, cast out demons. Freely you have received, freely give.
—MATTHEW 10:7–8

WE WERE WALKING DOWN THE AISLE AS A FAMILY ONE Sunday morning. We greeted people along the way, which was very typical for us. As we came to one of the couples whom we dearly love and look forward to seeing every Sunday, the husband said he had a horrible report from his doctor regarding his heart. We stopped right there, and my daughters and I began to pray to God to heal this man's heart. It was a quick prayer, and my youngest daughter led the last part of the prayer. We hugged him and his wife and then went to our seats.

We did not see the couple again until several weeks later, at which time, they stopped to talk to me at church, telling me that the husband's heart was 100 percent healed. He said that, after my daughter had prayed those weeks before, he had felt something happen inside his body. They had had evidence before the prayer of the horrific report, and then after the prayer he said they had seen a completely different heart and report. Honestly, I cannot even remember the simple prayer my daughter prayed. I just remember it was simple and direct and over in seconds. I also remember we had gone on about our day after praying for him, and my daughter had not even thought about it anymore.

God is the God of miracles and of mysteries. What I do know is we teach our children that it is possible for God to heal us. Before this healing, my daughter had seen God heal and change people's lives. She had also seen people not receive healing even after they had received prayer, yet she has not stopped believing. The reason she does not stop believing is because she has witnessed the truth of God before, and if He has done it before, He will do it again. In fact, in my daughter's school, when they report testimonies of God doing something, all the children chant, "Do it again, God! Do it again!" He did it, and He can do it again!

My husband is a history teacher, and He loves good, historical teaching and stories. History is important as we can learn from it, and hopefully, we will then not repeat the mistakes of those who have gone before us. What we can also learn from history is what is possible, and we can repeat the victories and the wins. One thing I have observed from being in our culture at Bethel Church is our leaders read and study the history of the Church. They pay attention to revival history. Those leaders who have gone before us understood God is able to do what He said He will do and do it again.

I grew up in church reading about all the stories in the Bible and honestly and full-heartedly believed that they were only for a time and a place—that they were limited to the people living in those times and places. Now that I am married to someone who loves to teach history where nations and leaders lead people into a better tomorrow due to what others have taught us, my thinking has drastically changed. It is almost as if most Christians read the Word of God as if it were a "dead" document of historical events. Instead, we know that the Word is alive, and it shows us what God can and will do again. We limit Bible history to good storytelling when it is so much more than that.

Why would there be a book like the Bible to document what can happen? Not to keep us entertained or to limit us to what was for a previous time. The Word of God is alive and breathing, and our God is alive and living now. He sent His Son so that we can relate to who He is and what He wants to do in us. So, we must teach our children about what God has done and teach them about what God can do. In our church, we spend a lot of time pressing in for healing in prayer, and we talk about it a lot. We spend a lot of time sharing testimonies of healings on many different levels—from physical to emotional and spiritual healing. This is why many people shift everything in their lives and travel from all over the world to get here to Bethel in Redding, California. We believe the impossible is possible, and we talk a lot about what we have seen God do. It consumes our culture. Even if we did not see a healing for something we pressed into, we do not let that one miss stop us from pressing more into healing from God. As Pastor Bill has said, "It fuels me even more to press into more healing." It is true. We will not stop believing in the impossible. We know that it is possible. The beautiful thing is our children hear about this truth, and they pray for it, and they see it. You cannot deny what you have actually seen with your own eyes and felt with your hands. God heals today, and we have a community of people who see it, believe it, and talk about it.

Creating a powerful faith culture requires that we tell each other about the stories of healing or breakthrough or salvations, that we gather together and make space to celebrate what God is doing, and that we press into what more God can do. To teach this culture to our children, we talk about God and what He can do. We also make space for our children to pray for others themselves. If I have a scratch, headache, stubbed toe, cut, or anything similar, I allow my children an opportunity to pray for me even with these seemingly insignificant things. I ask them if they know God can heal me, and they always say, "Yes!" Then they take a couple seconds and say, "Jesus . . . . Amen!" Then their next statement after prayer is, "Are you all better?" We establish such room for faith that immediately after the prayer there is a question asking for the result. I love it. If the result is nothing or a little something, then they pray again on their own. This is very common in our home, so much so that they ask each other to pray first for healing more than they commonly ask for a Band-Aid.

In our classes, we teach children to pray for each other. The teachers welcome children to come and lay hands on them and pray for them. We pray for leaders, families, communities, etc. We take time to ask God to do the impossible. We use toilet paper to wrap up our arms and legs in bandages, and in a posture of faith we break off the bandages from our bodies to declare God has healed us. We teach children that God is all-powerful and is able to do this for us today. When my daughters were younger, they would play raising each other from the dead. I recall playing tea party or tag when I was a child, but my daughters would gather with a group of friends and pray for each other as a game. One child pretended to be dead while the other children gathered around and prayed for the child to live and come back to life "in Jesus' name." Then the child who was dead would jump to her feet in excitement and say, "I am alive!" All the children would begin to jump up and down and run around, thanking Jesus for healing their friend. After a while, another child would want to take a turn at being raised from the dead. This would go on and on as they played outside. Can you imagine this being a game you see children playing? I never imagined this would entertain my children and their friends.

We just need to make space in our lives and in the lives of our children for things being made possible by faith. We as a family have experienced the loss of friends, family, and animals. In every situation we have prayed for healing. Not every time did we see healing as a result, but it does not stop us as a family from believing this is what God wants to do. We cannot explain why people or animals have not been healed when we prayed, but we do know who God is and what He will do and can do. If people or animals have not been healed, it is not because God did not care or want that. As a family, we talk about the nature of God. God is *our* Healer and deliverer. God is *with us*, Emmanuel. He does not leave us. Talking about this with your children is very important.

Disappointment is a real emotion in our journey in life, and pain typically is attached to disappointment. We make space to process this disappointment, but we make sure that we bring God into each area of our lives. The goal of the conversation is to bring our children back to the heart of the Father and to invite God to speak into our disappointment and pain even when we do not see the healing or receive the promise. Knowing that God is with us and He is for us is where we need to end our conversation with God. Talk about each time God did show up and what He did in the most unexpected times.

ACTIVATION

As a family, take time to study revivals like the Azusa Street revival or revivalists such as these:

1. John G. Lake

2. John Alexander Dowie

3. William Branham

4. Oral Roberts

5. Jack Coe

6. Aimee Semple McPherson

7. Kathryn Kuhlman

8. Billy Graham

Chapter 14

DECLARATIONS

Therefore it is of faith that it might be according to grace, so that the promise might be sure to all the seed, not only to those who are of the law, but also to those who are of the faith of Abraham, who is the father of us all.
—ROMANS 4:16

ONE SUNDAY NIGHT, WE HAD A LITTLE FIVE-YEAR-OLD BOY come in with an interesting creation he had made. He had taken a two-liter bottle and cut a slot on the side of it, had taken a string and tied it around two spots to wear the bottle over his shoulder like a bag, and had written a label on the outside of it which said he was raising money for the homeless. He brought this into class that evening, and the children in the class said they did not have any money to put in his bottle. So, they decided to make paper money from their classroom supplies and believed God would turn it into real money. And for the rest of the classroom time, the children colored and drew different denominations of money and deposited it into this boy's bottle bag that he had made. The class knew this act would create great expectation for what God would do.

Later in the month, the boy said people would see him wearing it around and would ask questions about it. When they heard what the kids in the classroom did, the adults were so moved that they began putting real money into the bottle bag. The teachers asked the boy to ask God to whom he was to give this money. And the little boy did. He later told the teachers God had shown him a picture of a man. According to the picture, the man was older and had an eye patch. The boy decided to actually draw a picture of the man. That very week, the boy found this homeless man with an eye patch and gave him the picture and the money that he had raised for him.

Have you ever had to remind yourself of the truth so that your inner dialogue or life circumstance did not end up being the thing influencing you? We have all had to do this many times to help us navigate through our day. As a parent of a newborn, I had to remind myself that the sleepless nights were not forever, that it was only a stage of development for my babies. I also had to teach myself that the cries of my baby were simply a form of communication from her to me as her mother. I had to separate my fatigue and my emotions from the truth that my baby needed something, and we were learning from each other in the early stages of life. Then I had to learn to understand my toddler as she learned language and self-reliance and independence with me as a parent who had knowledge to share with and impart to her. My toddler's desire to become independent to maneuver through life, doing what she wanted apart from my influence, was a dance we had to learn together. At every stage—from baby to toddler to adolescent—my children had to go through a developmental process to learn to be powerful. As the parent of each developmental stage, my job was to reinforce their identity and ground them in truth and relationship.

Through all the stages of development, we use declarations to reinforce identity, truth, and connection. We use biblical truth and put it on our lips to speak over ourselves or our children, reminding us and them that what we are experiencing may not be our final destinations. To keep us on the journey to our destination, we ever keep in front of us why we are on this journey to our destination. We may hear or think getting to where we are going is impossible, but as Luke 18:27 says, *"All things are possible."* We may think, "I cannot do it." Philippians 4:13 tells us something else: *"I can do all things through Christ who strengthens me."* We may think, "I cannot go on," but 2 Corinthians 12:9 says, *"My grace is sufficient for you."* These Scriptures are all declarations. They give us fortitude, which is courage in pain, to keep moving forward. They continue to define our why and reinforce our identity. If we can teach our children to put truth over their circumstances—to make and believe these declarations—on a consistent basis, then this becomes a tool that they will use in life as they continue to encounter adversity.

God is enough, God sees us, God wants us to succeed, God wants a relationship with us, God chooses us, God forgives us, and God loves us. We can believe and declare such things about our God and keep going. This is another example of how foundational God's Word is to our growth and maturity. We use God's truth to hardwire our brains to differentiate the real truth from the feelings or appearances associated with our circumstances.

Proverbs 18:21 says, *"Death and life are in the power of the tongue, and those who love it will eat its fruit."* Our words can bring life, or they can bring death. Words and beliefs can shift and change the course and direction our lives. Speaking truth over others and ourselves helps to bring clarity of mind and thought. It brings encouragement and strength to our hearts and minds. It also allows us to increase our faith to partner with truth rather than react to what we may be experiencing in the moment. We must shift our approach and become proactive in our thoughts, hearts, and minds, instead of being reactive. Many people now are living their lives reacting to what is coming at them. If we create a foundation of truth in our lives, then we can use it like a bank. We can make withdrawals from it to respond to what is currently happening to us. This creates a rich, whole, and faith-filled people who walk in wisdom and truth.

Partnering with God's Word which is alive and working now in our lives means we are inviting the Holy Spirit into our thoughts, hearts, and minds. The reason God's Word is alive is because of the Holy Spirit moving over the words and truth. He is counseling and ministering to us, and we are actively connecting to the Holy Spirit in relationship to Him.

ACTIVATION

Write down a family declaration. This should be something that you feel is unique and appropriate to your family, perhaps identifying why God chose each of you to be together. Once you write this out together, then find a way to display this so you all can see it and visit it often.

Here is a suggested format on how to write this declaration:

1. Find a verse to serve as the basis for your family declaration. Some great examples are: Deuteronomy 3:16; Isaiah 41:10; Jeremiah 29:11; Matthew 17:20; Mark 10:27; Romans 8:28; 15:13; Philippians 4:13. Find one that fits you!

2. What has God called your family to be?

3. Who do you have in your family that is unique in their call?

4. What do you want to establish with your family on this earth?

5. What is your hope for your family?

6. What is God's promise to your family?

7. What is God saying over your family?

You will find this fun for your family to discover a declaration over your home, your lives, and what God has called you to do. You could pass this on to the next generations to come. I pray that this will be a fun journey to discover who you are as a family and declare and pray this over your home.

Chapter 15

SPIRITUAL GIFTS

There are diversities of gifts, but the same
Spirit. There are differences of ministries, but
the same Lord. And there are diversities of
activities, but it is the same God who works
all in all. But the manifestation of the Spirit
is given to each one for the profit of all.
—1 CORINTHIANS 12:4–7

IN CHAPTER 1, I HAD MENTIONED ABOUT MY ELDEST DAUGH-ter who would see Jesus, angels, and even demonic beings when she was only two years old. As her parents, both my husband and I had not experienced anything like this before, so we were unsure as to how to raise her or even help her in this process. What we found helpful in this journey was to ask her a lot of questions and find out how to navigate through things with her. She was dealing with a lot of fear, which I completely understood. She also was struggling to tell us every time she was encountering the Lord or an angel or a demon because she did not know that we were not seeing what she was seeing. We would see the fear on her face and have to figure out the source of it. Eventually, we found out the fear came from the scary or supernatural things she was seeing. And that's why we had to ask her questions for clarity.

We had to learn that our daughter's normal was not everyone else's normal. We also had to understand that her language was limited due to her age. During this journey, as I had mentioned before in chapter 1, we found an adult, my friend from church, who had experienced similar encounters. She was helpful to us as parents who had no experience in this area. We could ask her questions and receive insights on how to handle our daughter or how to respond to our daughter's feelings. An important tool or truth we also found with our daughter was teaching her that she was powerful in this gift. We told her how God chose her to see things in a different realm. We encouraged her to ask God why He gave her this gift. We taught her that she has authority over the demonic beings and even the angels, her voice was important, and she could tell the demonic beings to leave and ask the angels why they were there with her. Furthermore, we encouraged her that, if Jesus came to her, then she should talk to Him. This was a journey, and we did not handle everything perfectly, but we learned a lot as a family and a lot about our daughter.

It's amazing how beautiful God has made each individual. Not only did He give us different personalities that express themselves in our thoughts, desires, opinions, and interests, but He also gave each one of us spiritual gifts such as wisdom, knowledge, faith, healing, miracles, prophecy, distinguishing spirits, speaking in tongues, and interpretation. All of these are important to discover so that we can know and understand who we are and what we have been created to give the world and people around us. We are enriching the families, communities, and societies that we all get to be a part of. We each have a purpose, and our gifts and missions are different from each other's. We are designed to bring value to each family, community, and environment we are a part of. This should be exciting as we begin to discover not only who we are and what gifts we have, but also to discover who God has given us in our children and what gifts they have to display to the world.

Knowing what gifts each of your children carry is a great start in helping to bring their gifts to maturity. This can be hard to accomplish, but I am challenging families to aim for a starting place and not for perfection. I think if our approach is to learn and discover and give our family freedom to learn and expect to make mistakes, then we will be able to free ourselves from a fear of failure. One way to look at this is we are on a journey to discover who we are and who we have. Journeys take time and attention. There is a time to watch and observe, to ask questions, and a time to take some risk and see if your thoughts or observations are right or wrong. Each part of this journey and discovery is experimental. We get to learn through success and through failure. Learning who we are and who we have is the aim.

Our lives are designed for discovery, and we learn as we go. We have the best tool in our journey in life: the Lord and His Spirit! This creates space for the Lord and His Spirit to co-labor with us. Think of it like figuring out what your children's interests are. Whether it be music, sports, art, academia—you name it—once you find a category they are interested in, there is even more to discover within the category. Take music, for example. Your children's interests or gifts could include playing a certain instrument, writing music, singing, studying music history, or conducting. There is so much more to be discovered, and it is a learning experience and journey. So, as you discover your own gifts with the Lord, give the same grace to your children as you help learn and discover the gifts God has given them.

The Bible says to *"earnestly desire spiritual gifts"* (1 Cor. 11:23). This is more than just wishful thinking. It is positioning your heart and mind to believe that these gifts have already been given and all you need to do is use them. For example, in our house, when our children get hurt, our first reaction is always to pray. When we pray, we pray as if it is God's will that they be healed, then we check it. Something like, "Lord, we just ask for complete healing and all the pain to leave, in Jesus' name. Amen! All better?" For my younger ones, this set an expectation that, when we pray, things happen. We need not stop at healing. This is for all the spiritual gifts.

Kids need a model of how to approach and use their spiritual gifts. While we might find it easier to model good character, the Lord has called us to much more than that. As our pastor, Bill Johnson, often says, God has called us to the impossible. As a result, it is our job as their parents to position ourselves for reliance on God. It's possible that you have no idea what the spiritual gifts listed in the New Testament mean. That's not a problem. The Holy Spirit is called our

Counselor, and He guides us in all things. Ask Him, and He will show you how to walk them out. If at first you do not hear Him, keep asking. This is our posture and response. We need to know we can call on Him and He will answer us. This doesn't mean that everything you hear will have the weight of Scripture. And it also doesn't mean you won't make some mistakes along the way, but it is the Holy Spirit's joy to walk us through modeling and using our gifts as we pursue our relationship with Him.

Just a quick note on the fivefold ministry mentioned in Ephesians. Kris Vallotton, our associate senior pastor, has often mentioned that the fivefold leaders are called for the "equipping of the saints." While titles are not important, recognizing the gifts in your leaders will go a long way in preparing your own house. Leaders who function as apostles, prophets, evangelists, pastors, and teachers will influence people with these gifts. The gift that they have is something that their life breathes naturally and does not need to be exclaimed or shouted. Sitting under anyone's leadership that carries a gift of an evangelist will extend its influence and anointing over you. So, if your children or you as a parent have one of these gifts, your family will be influenced by the gift in their own lives. Think of some churches as an example. Some are great at discipling, others at evangelizing, and still other churches at seeing miracles, signs, and wonders. When you think of these churches that have such strength in an area, it is most likely because their leaders operate in this gift in their lives.

I am simply going to run through different gifts found in God's Word. There are gifts in ministry, manifestation gifts, and motivational gifts. All believers take part in these gifts in various ways. There are gifts of the Holy Spirit: wisdom, word of knowledge, faith, gifts of healing, miracles, prophecy, discerning spirits, tongues, and interpretation of tongues. Ephesians 4 talks about the ministering gifts or the fivefold ministry: apostles, prophets, teachers, preachers, and evangelists. In Romans 12, we learn of motivational gifts of the Spirit: prophecy, serving, teaching, encouraging, giving, leading, and showing mercy.

Each category of gifts is how God ministers to us (motivational), speaks to others through us (ministry), and how His power is expressed through us (manifestation). This is not an area any of us will become experts in by any means. I am simply putting this before myself and you to see that, through relationship with God and your family, you can identify who you have. When we can see a little more clearly who we have in our family and homes, then we can help lead and minister and grow together with God and our family together. Taking time to discover and grow yourself is beautiful, but inviting your family into the process together is life-changing.

ACTIVATION

1. Get a notebook or journal for each of your family members.

2. Take time to note and write in them for each other what spiritual gifts you see. For example, you as a mother or father write in your notebook for your children what they did or said that connects to a spiritual gift. Note in that journal or notebook every time you have noticed your children speak, operate, or manifest a gift from God. If your child shared Jesus with a friend that day at school, write this down in their journal. You can even note the gifting like "evangelist" next to it. If your child wants to pray over people who are sick, write this down in their journal and note the gifting by writing "healing" or "apostle." You can go back into the journals throughout the days, months, and years, should you keep up the practice, and see if you can notice a common thread of gifts in their lives. Doing this together as a family will cause you each to take notice of how God is moving in you and through your lives.

Chapter 16

PARENTS AND HOME

As for me and my house we will serve the Lord.
—JOSHUA 24:15B

ONE OF OUR DAUGHTERS CAME TO US ONE TIME AND TOLD US that she had spent time with God in worship. She said He was speaking to her about who she was and why He made her. She explained to us that God had told her what she was going to do as a job. We were so excited to hear what God told her and could not wait to hear. We asked her, "What did He say?"

She was very excited to say, "He said I was going to be a waitress!"

To be honest, I was pretty disappointed in that response, so I said, "I think He told you that would be your first job."

My husband chimed in and asked my daughter, "Why do you think God said you were going to be a waitress?"

147

She was very quick to reply, "Because they love to help people get what they need and want. They serve people and talk to them, and then they go and grab the items they need."

At that moment, it became clear to me that maybe God was showing her a job she could identify that pointed to her overall purpose. She was able to see one person's role in another person's life. I can now see that my daughter is naturally a person who loves to serve others and thinks of others. She is also such a steadfast and loyal friend to everyone she meets that this type of job and role would be easy for her to walk into.

Finding out more about the why of our words, experiences, or relationships in dialogue with God is fascinating to me. We should not just jump to our own conclusions or understanding without pressing into asking more questions from God and others that can bring more vision and clarity. This is what our relationship with God and each other should look like. This posture helps us to grow in our connection and relationship with each other.

I think one of the biggest mistakes that a parent can make is to set the bar higher for their children than they have set it for themselves. An often quoted Scripture from Ephesians 6:1 is the edict for children to obey their parents. What is not cited as often is verse 4 of the same chapter that instructs fathers not to exasperate their children. In the King James Version, it says *"provoke not your children to wrath."* Probably the reason it is not cited as often is that it seems an impossible task to keep your teenagers from getting offended at even the smallest thing.

To understand teenagers and why they get angry is not as hard as it seems at first. As parents, all we actually need to do is to take an honest look at ourselves. It does not happen to us as often now, but can you remember the last time you were confronted about something you did that someone else found unacceptable? Think back to a time in your youth that you reacted to an adult's disapproval. Might I suggest you were probably defensive. You may have even been offended. Did you find yourself looking through your memory trying to recall each action of the person that confronted you? What is defensiveness? What is an offense?

Offense is a natural reaction. It speaks to a desire that is put inside of us by God when He created us in His image; it is the desire to be free. It's the part of us that has free will. As we grow in the Lord, we start to learn that what felt like freedom when we were younger often is just bondage by another name. It is harder to see this when you are young because many of your choices are desire-driven instead of vision-driven.

Vision-driven is what we are supposed to be. Romans 12:2 says, *"Do not be conformed to this world, but be transformed by the renewing of your mind."* In this verse, there is first a passive position which is what happens when you do nothing—you conform. Then later in the verse, there is an active position, which is the renewing of the mind. The active position is what leads us to transformation. Renewing your mind requires you to set out to do something, an action, and in this case, you begin to think about God's thoughts. This is the beginning of the process that changes you. This is what maturity and wisdom in relationship with God does for us. We can assume that this is easier to say than do. It is difficult for teenagers to do, but realistically this is difficult for all of us to do. It is possible to do because God calls us to this place in our mindsets and relationships.

I think for many of us we have not been intentional about thinking God's thoughts. Rather, we followed the patterns set before us. The patterns can come from our families, society, communities, even every part of our world. For example, we went to school, did our homework, graduated, found a job, got married, and had kids. Inherently, none of these things are bad, but they are patterns set out by the world and culture that are easy to follow. Following the world doesn't require much vision, just conforming to the norm that is set in front of us.

The result of following the pattern set before you without thinking about it is that we never get the value of things in this life and can discard them the moment we have a chance. How many of us have discarded learning as a phase of life. We did what was asked of us by our teachers, knowing that this was just something we had to do. We didn't necessarily put any vision or application to the learning. We simply followed through with the motions. The end result of all this is that, when you start forcing your kids to do the same things you have in the same pattern or order, you are teaching them that those things have to be done but really don't have any value. Any of this type of mindset can cause offense or resentment whether you are aware of it or not. When children are forced to do chores, complete homework, pay bills, do a job you do not like, then they can point to you with resentment. They can begin to feel stuck in life and resent you for it. How can we pursue vision from God but still live in this world? It is a promise He has for us when we are intentional in living and meditating on His words and are pursuing our relationship with Him.

Anything worth doing is worth repeating. This holds true with everything in life, including our relationships with Christ. I don't hold my kids to a standard I do not hold myself to. My kids need to see my relationship with God. For example, in our house, worship music is played from the living room first thing in the morning each day so that, when they enter the common area, it's the first thing they hear. In fact, this will become something my children will come to expect and will find it odd if worship music is not played in the common area of our home in the mornings. They will even grow to miss it and crave it.

Another thing we do as a family is, in the evenings after dinner, we spend twenty minutes reading the Bible together, everyone having his or her own Bible, whether it be the graphic novel for the younger ones or an art Bible for the older one. There is no requirement to read a certain amount, no requirement to read really, just to have the Bible out and be quiet in the living room together. Since we've started doing this, what we've found is that our kids are quick to ask questions about what they are reading, leading to some great discussions. This has become a great value for molding our children into valuing the Word of God in our lives.

ACTIVATION

1. Read the Bible together as a family! Take some time to get everyone their own age-appropriate Bible, or watch a clip of the Bible project on YouTube together.

2. Then take some time to share with each other what you have heard or maybe discuss something your children needed clarity about.

3. Take time as a family to process a biblical truth, a miracle you don't have faith for, or a reason God chose to do something, and talk about it. Here are some topics to consider if you need a bit more help on what to discuss together as a family:

- Genesis 1, "Creation": Who made God? God has no beginning or end. He has always existed.

- 1 Samuel 3, "God speaks to Samuel": Can God speak to me? Yes, He can speak to through His voice, His Word, others speaking to us, and many other ways.

- John 3:16, "God loves the world": How do I know if God loves everyone?

- Genesis 2–3, "Adam and Eve": Why did Adam and Eve sin?

- Matthew 10, "Healing": Can someone be healed today? What did Jesus command His disciples to do? What has Jesus asked His disciples to do for the world?

Chapter 17

TESTIMONIES

However, Jesus did not permit him, but said to him, "Go home to your friends, and tell them what great things the Lord has done for you, and how He has had compassion on you."
—MARK 5:19

THIS SECTION IS DESIGNED TO GIVE YOU SPARKS OF HOPE. IT'S meant to show you what is possible for you in your home with your children. I have taken some of the testimonies from adults in our immediate and greater communities who have submitted their testimonies of what God has done with their children. As you read through these testimonies, believe that God can and will do them again for you and your children in your homes.

Testimonies are meant to encourage and bring hope to others who need to hear of what God can do. We tell our testimonies because we want the world to know that God is able and willing to move in the midst of our lives.

Cancer Tap: Rick Larson, California, USA

I was diagnosed with stage IV esophageal cancer in 2008. My son wanted us to go the Bethel healing rooms in Redding, but at the time I was not a believer and did not want to go. As the diagnosis hit me and my fiancé, we decided to go.

As we entered the healing rooms, I was struck by what I saw. I had never seen a place with so much love, and I felt hope. I will never forget I had my one son praying for me on my one side, my younger son praying for me on my other side, and my fiancé praying behind me.

Suddenly, a twelve-year-old boy came bouncing toward me and said, "Rich Larson?"

Immediately, I was really mad, and I thought to myself, You have got to be kidding me! I drove five and a half hours, I am sick with cancer, and I have got a little boy to pray for me! I need Benny Hinn; I need pastor Bill Johnson; I need somebody anointed. Is everyone out for lunch?

The next thing I knew, I felt this Presence coming over me, and I remember thinking, *He is going to knock me over!* I had specifically written on my healing rooms paperwork, "Do not touch me," but this boy, uninhibited, had come up and tapped me on the chest, and I went crashing down onto the ground under the power of God.

After forty-five minutes, I finally woke up on the carpet with a pillow under my head.

In disbelief, I was just lying there, and the little boy was rubbing my chest. He said, "How are you feeling, Rick?"

Looking at the boy, I said, "Do you know what? My fear is gone!"

The boy shouted, "Hallelujah!"

There was a lady praying with the little boy, and she asked me, "Rick, how do you feel inside?"

As I became aware of my body, I said, "I feel like something has happened inside!" I replied in amazement. "I can feel warmth."

When I saw my family, I remember them saying, "Dad, you have got color!"

I began to feel hungry and heavy. I knew then that it was done, that I was healed, and that God had done something for me! I could not understand how or why He did it, but I knew He did.

I went back to the doctor, and when he went to take the X-rays of my esophagus, he said they were having trouble with the X-ray machine. I looked at the three images, and there was a beam of light coming out of the center of each of the pictures.

I called my son and told him about the pictures, and he began to cry. He said to me, "Dad! Those are the pictures of God. His Word says that He is the light, and He was in your throat, Dad! He was probably really busy. If He had known they were taking a picture, He probably would have turned around and smiled!"

Today, I serve in the Bethel healing rooms, and there is no cancer anywhere in my body. Not only that, but God healed my blood pressure completely, and I can still eat fast food!

Dancing Encounters: Kiana Mattson, California, USA

My name is Kiana, I am nine years old, and I love to dance! One day, I was dancing with my little sister in the healing rooms ministry in our church. I saw a team leader praying for a man. We found out later the man had back pain, but the team leader was not seeing any progress for his healing. When she saw us dancing, God told her to have us come and dance over the man with the back pain.

So, my sister and I went and danced around the man. Almost immediately, he went right into an encounter with God and fell flat on the floor. It was surprising to him because he had never had an encounter with God before. God's presence was so strong that the team leader said she could hardly stand.

It made me feel really happy and thankful that God could use my little sister and me as we did what we loved to do!

"You Will Live and Not Die": Ginny Grimes, California, USA

Our family dog, Molly, was throwing up and had horrible diarrhea. When we took her to the vet, the vet said she had swallowed something and would need surgery to remove whatever was blocking her intestines. The surgery would cost a few thousand dollars, and we did not have the money.

We were praying for the blockage to come out on its own, but days went by, and Molly was not improving. I was feeding her with a syringe, but there was still no progress.

One night before bed, I told our four children to say goodbye to Molly because she was not going to live through the night. Three of them crowded around her and instantly started crying. Justus, our four-year-old little boy, came over and said, "Hey guys, why are your crying? We should be praying!" He then started speaking in tongues and praying.

One of our girls started singing the most beautiful song in the Spirit. Our other two girls started to intensely declare, "Molly, you will live and not die. Molly, we speak life into your body. Molly, Jesus is making you new!" This went on for minutes as my husband and I stood in awe at the faith of our children.

I asked Jesus what I should do, and I felt like I was supposed to call Molly to the back door even thought I knew she had not moved for days. I said, "Molly, come!" and she jumped right up! She ran straight out the door, did two laps around our backyard, and then squatted and pooped out the stinkiest, big old rock! She came inside, ate, and drank, and she is still living today!

Provision with Prayer: Redding, CA

As my thirteen-year-old daughter and I prayed, she had a prayer and asked God for checks in the mail each Tuesday for our family. Before the first Tuesday had hit, I was looking at my email, and I noticed one from our bank. The email stated that someone had deposited $2,000 into our bank account.

Fast forward to the following Tuesday, and I had another notification in my email that we received a $1,000 refund!

God does crazy stuff to blow our minds! Our kids' prayers are no less powerful than our prayers as adults. In fact, we know we are meant to be more childlike as Jesus said. So, next time you want to pray for something, find a child around you, and let them release their prayer of faith over your situation.

Drawing God's Love: A Six-Year-Old's Encounter with God: Redding, CA

Since quarantine started, life at home had been a bit wild with two young boys. I've become a homeschool mom overnight, so it's been challenging for me to find time with Jesus, let alone teach my kids. One morning, though, I was in my room spending some time with the Lord. My husband was making breakfast in the kitchen with the boys when our six-year-old came into our bedroom. He saw me there with my Bible and journal, and he heard the worship music playing in the background. He asked what I was doing. I explained that I was spending time with the Lord. He wanted to come and join me, so we sat in bed together.

Then he asked what I was writing about in my journal. Surprised by his sudden interest, I shared with him a little about what Jesus had been telling me. We then lay together, listening to worship. My six-year-old focused on drawing a picture of a globe. When I asked him about it, he explained that the picture was about people all over the world coming to know Jesus. To my surprise, he quoted John 3:16 and then proceeded to explain the other aspects of the picture. There were angels being released all over the globe to bring healing for the coronavirus, Jesus' blood was being poured out onto the world, and there were swirls of color that he described as "the holy wind from Jesus' wing of protection."

This was not the normal vocabulary of our house, so I knew my six-year-old was having an encounter with Jesus. He looked at me with tears in his eyes and said, "Mom, I'm so happy, I think I might cry."

We continued to lay there together as he experienced the presence of God. He asked me to read the Bible out loud to him, so I read some of the Psalms I'd been reading.

Afterward, he said, "When Jesus comes, my heart feels so big. It feels as big as my body."

I was blown away. Most days, as a parent—especially during quarantine—I'm just hoping my kids survive until the evening. But to see my son encounter the Lord for himself was the greatest gift. I have always prayed Isaiah 54:13 over my boys, *"Your children will be taught by the Lord."* And, that morning I got to see that promise become a reality. There is no greater joy.

Dancing with Jesus: A Five-Year-Old's Experience with Jesus

During the last month or so, with everything locked down due to the coronavirus, my five-year-old has been having very impactful experiences with Jesus and the Holy Spirit. I've come into his room at night to tuck him into bed, only to realize that he's been having a conversation with Jesus on his own. He has been in such a tender place after these conversations that he's felt very emotional as his heart is touched by the Holy Spirit.

Over Easter, we had been talking as a family about what had happened to Jesus on Good Friday and what Easter was all about. My five-year-old had felt so moved with compassion that, while he was playing outside, he dropped down onto his knees and began to pray. Later, he told me, "Mom, I was praying that everyone would love Jesus and know what He did on Easter." His heart has been so stirred for evangelism.

One of the most beautiful experiences he's had this past month, though, was during a normal day at home. We had some worship music playing in the background and he was dancing around. Suddenly, he came running up to me and said, "Mom, I love to dance!"

I responded, "Yeah, buddy, I love to dance, too. It makes my body feel so good."

In a serious tone, he said, "No, Mom, when I dance with Jesus, my heart feels so happy. I just feel His love so much." I wasn't aware of the powerful encounter with Jesus he was having in that moment, but he wanted me to understand what dancing with Jesus meant to him.

New Knees: Prayer from My Son with an Abundant Blessing

My son was diagnosed with Sensory Process Disorder, which caused his speech to be very slow and delayed.

I have had knee pain ever since I was born. I eventually went to see a doctor, and after a scan, they diagnosed me with

Patellofemoral Pain Syndrome. I stopped complaining about it or mentioning it to anyone because there was not much that the doctor could do, and after a lot of rehabilitation, the pain had not gone away.

One day, when my son was three-and-a-half years old, I went to pick him up from school. When we got home, we sat on the couch, and I asked him about his day. He looked at me and asked, "Mama, do you have an ouchie?"

I said to him, "No, I don't have an ouchie," and asked him again about his day. However, he persisted in asking again if I had pain in my knee.

Again, I said no, but then I heard the Holy Spirit say, "Listen to him. There is something that I want to do." So, I said, "Yes, Mama has an ouchie."

Without me showing him where, he stood up, walked right up to me and tapped my injured knee and asked if he could see. Then he rolled up my pants to just above my knee, and he put his hands on my knee. My husband and I can't actually remember ever teaching him how to pray for the sick, but he went straight into it. His hands felt like they were on fire! He then started talking to God, but I did not understand what he was saying. He finished talking and looked up at me, smiled, and walked away.

My knee felt really hot, and I felt like God said, "Test it!" So, I decided to get up and check out if I had pain. Incredibly, for the first time I had no pain at all! I did a squat, and still I had no pain! My boy prayed for my healing, and I was completely healed! Maybe he was even speaking in tongues without my knowing.

Shortly after this miracle, my son began to speak normally and was healed of Sensory Process Disorder.

Children's Prayer while Playing in a Park

We had arrived at a park to meet one of our friends. When we saw her, she had a young mum and two daughters with her. She asked if we would pray for her friend because she had fibromyalgia.

I looked at the two girls and felt to tell them the testimony of a man in Mexico who had his knees and hips healed when I'd had three guys who didn't know Jesus pray for him. I had told the guys to pray, "Jesus, heal him." I looked at the girls and said, "Would you like to heal Mum?"

They said, "Yes!"

So, they put their hands on their mum and prayed a simple prayer, "Jesus, heal Mum!" Before they'd even finished, it was like someone unseen had punched their mother to the ground! I was shocked as she crashed onto the grass in this public setting. She was shaking and trembling, and I asked, "Are you okay? Are you okay?" She trembled under the power of God as we watched Jesus do His work.

The next day when we were sharing testimonies at a meeting, this young mother stood up and said that she'd had the first full night of sleep and first time waking up pain-free in over two years! She could also raise her arms for the first time free of pain. The fibromyalgia was gone! Do it again, Jesus!

After-School Program with Healings and Salvation

Jesus has radically loved the elementary school kids in our after-school program all year! A few weeks into the academic year, we were teaching the kids that God is in a good mood and that He heals people's bodies when we ask Him. During snack time, before the lesson, we asked if any of the kids needed prayer.

After hearing "my cat is sick" and "my dog ran away," a little boy said his back hurt. On a scale of one to ten, his pain was "at a 90." All the kids rallied around him and quickly released healing over him. The look of shock when he realized his back didn't hurt anymore was priceless. That day, 23 kids were healed of physical problems that ranged from hurt ankles to eczema.

We prayed for a little girl's grandma who was in the hospital. The grandma was supposed to be in the hospital for another week, but the day after we prayed, she was able to go home. The seven-year-old girl told her, "I know why you came home from the hospital early." The little girl explained that we had prayed for her grandma at school the day before, and that God heals people when we pray because He's in a good mood. Then she told her the story of Jesus and how He gave everything for her, and the girl led her grandma to Jesus for the first time! A few months later, the grandma passed away. She is with Jesus right now because a little girl encountered the goodness of God and brought that encounter home with her.

After God showed up and demonstrated His goodness to the kids, we intended to teach them how Jesus' blood paid for everything. Before the lesson, we mentioned Jesus' name in conversation, and one of the little boys asked, "Jesus? Who is Jesus? I have a cousin named Jesuís, but I've never heard of Jesus."

After hearing about what Jesus did, God encountered them all through a vision where Jesus took away their bad things and gave them His good things. That day, 22 kids, including the little boy who had never heard of Jesus, gave their hearts to Him.

A week doesn't go by without one of the kids being healed in their body or someone deciding to choose joy in a sad situation. This Thursday a little girl told us, "My mommy and daddy fight a lot, but now I just pray, and Jesus makes it all better."

Sticky Note Provisions

I moved to Redding ten years ago with my four kids, and we had nothing but backpacks. By the grace of God, we found a rental and slowly began to rebuild our lives. The kids had been through loss and abuse. The situation created a real need within us to pray.

Unbeknownst to me, my eight-year-old son was praying for signs that God existed. One afternoon, he came running up to me yelling, "God's not answering my prayers!" Being a single mom with four small kids meant I was always answering a considerable number of questions. I had explanations and teachings for every question. However, when my son asked me why God would not answer, it was not a teaching moment. It was important that my son see God show up.

I called my kids together, and, handing them two sticky notes each, I instructed them to write down a prayer on each one and put the notes on the door in the hallway.

The prayers ranged from small to large. I commissioned my children to pray the prayers on the notes every time they walked by the door. When a prayer had been answered, I'd pull the note off the door, leaving a blank spot to indicate God had answered that prayer.

Over the months, the notes came off the door one by one, restoring faith, until there was only one left. The last note read, "a car for mommy." This note was written by my eight-year-old son. That note remained for quite a while and lost its stickiness. We put tape on and continued re-taping. We were relentless in our prayers to have that note come down.

One day, I was at the table when a set of keys landed in front of me. A friend of mine had come over as a surprise to give me a paid-off car! They had no idea we were praying for one. My son came home from school, I walked him down the hall, and I asked him to take off the last note. He cried. He wasn't crying over a car; he was crying in restored faith. God showed up.

Children's prayers are fierce. But so is their doubt at times. Sometimes we need to set teaching aside and ask God for action.

Beni Johnson says, "God is not bound to act according to what we believe about Him. Rather, we are bound to believe Him as He demonstrates Himself to us."

Children Create Their Own Bible Study: Redding, California

This year, our children's school campus is closed to parents, so I started meeting with a couple moms at the church across the street to pray for the school once a week on Wednesdays. The kids are split up into pods (small groups) and play zones during recess.

One Wednesday morning, one of my daughter's friends knows that my daughter is a Christian and goes to Bethel, and she mentioned to her that, while her family was not Christian, she has an aunt who gave her a Bible. My daughter's friend wanted to know if my daughter wanted to read their Bibles together at school! My daughter said *yes* and brought her Bible to school the next day! Her friend forgot hers, but my daughter said, "That's okay! I can just read mine!" So, she started reading it out loud at recess and a bunch of girls started coming around saying, "I love this story!" Or "My mom has a Bible, too!"

This led them to start a Bible club during morning recess, and my daughter set them up on a rotation to take turns reading and take turns praying. I asked her if all of her friends have prayed before, and she said she didn't know, but they are now! She also said one day instead of reading the Bible she was going to teach them what she learned at children's camp about forgiveness.

It's so powerful that the Lord inspired these sixth-grade girls to read the Bible out loud on their public school campus, and they are praying together! Just another gift of this season. God is on the move always!

Special Needs Testimonies from Our Classrooms at Church: Redding, CA

In our class, we've had a visitor for the last three weeks. She's a precious six-year-old girl with Down syndrome who loves to love and also pray for people. After the first Sunday that she came, here's what her mom wrote: "Tonight she talked in sentences all night long. She talked more this evening than she usually says in a month. At one point I asked her who she was talking to and she said, 'Jesus.' She told me, 'He came to help all of us mommy. It's going to be okay, we are safe, we are loved.'" Thank You, Jesus!

A thirteen-year-old boy in our class comes to the healing rooms almost every Saturday and typically plays by the wall the entire time. Last month's update had a picture of him painting in the healing rooms for the first time. This past Saturday, he briefly joined our children's healing team again. This time, he drew a picture of the face of an eagle, and after prompting him, he said that it meant, "Always be strong, even in dark times." He quickly tossed it in the direction of the man he wanted to give it to and started to move on. His leader for the day brought the teenaged boy back over to the man and asked him if the eagle meant anything. He looked at it for a while and shared that maybe God is asking the man to arise out of some situations in his life. Then the leader asked if the man had any pain, and the man pointed to his right knee. The leader and this teenager put the drawing of the eagle on the man's knee two to three times, and all the pain in his knee left! We talked to this young boy later, and he smiled and said how Jesus healed a man's knee through his art. Then he stated that he wished Jesus would heal his own back as it was feeling really tight. Moments later, he was bending backwards, free of pain and the tension in his back! Thank You, Jesus!

Chapter 18

CHILDREN'S MINISTRY LEADERS

*All this is for your benefit, so that the grace
that is reaching more and more people may
cause thanksgiving to overflow to the glory
of God. Therefore we do not lose heart.*
—2 CORINTHIANS 4:15–16 NIV

IF YOU HAVE WORKED OR ARE WORKING IN CHILDREN'S MINIS-
try, I wanted to spend some time thanking you and encouraging you. Whether you are in the Church or outside the Church
reaching different groups of children for God, this section is
specifically aimed at and geared toward you. God has placed
you to reach children outside their homes. This is a privilege
and honor to be able to be entrusted with the care of children
and to bring supplemental strength to their spirits and relationships with God. You may minister to children who do
not have homes, and you help build up these children spiritually. You may have children for whom you care who come

from all walks of life. They may or may not be Christian. But I want you to know that you play an important role. Thank you for doing your part and working so hard to edify, encourage, strengthen, and build a relationship with each and every child that you have in your care.

Your role is not to be taken lightly. I tell all my team and families in my church that this is ministry—no matter the age, the time, or the space. We have been given this role, and we make sure we steward our time well with God. When we have children in our care, we have God speaking over us, we have the children with us, and we invite the Holy Spirit to guide and counsel us through our time with each child.

I don't know about you, but my love for the Church was a gift my parents instilled in me. In fact, I feel like my church is just as much "family" and "home" to me as my real family and real home. Church and children's ministry have been such a part of my life that I went to college to get my degree to be a children's pastor. I don't know why you are involved in working and ministering to children, but one thing I do know, your ministry to children is meaningful. It is valuable, and I want to thank you again for investing in lives of children for God's glory. As you invest in current generations, you are also investing in future generations. This is how you steward revival. It must be passed on from one generation to the next. Revival can be sustained, and this is how we can do our part to sustain it. Thank you for doing your part, and in the pages that follow, I hope to encourage you in your ministry to children.

Chapter 19

MINISTRY NOT CHILDCARE

*It is easier to build strong children
than to repair broken men.*
—FREDERICK DOUGLAS

MY PARENTS WERE FOSTER PARENTS TO OVER ONE HUNDRED children in the span of fifteen years. It was so heartbreaking to see children come into our homes those very first moments. The children came with very little of anything that they owned or that reminded them of who they were. These were children whose eyes had seen terrifying things, whose bodies had endured horrific environments, and whose little hearts had felt devastating heartbreak.

Every child who came into our home always wanted to go back to their homes with their parents. Children are conditioned to love, and they are created to love the ones who birthed them into this world, even though they may be in broken environments. I have, however, watched several children walk out of their brokenness into wholeness because of

Jesus. Statistically, though, that is not the case for most children. Jesus is the answer to our world, and introducing children to Jesus as early as we possibly can is the most life-altering experience we can ever bring to children let alone any adult.

Oftentimes, churches will wait to invest their time and energy to pursue and establish real authentic relationships with our children when they are in youth ministry. Our children are around twelve years of age when we really tell them about God or Jesus. Maybe if you are in a church that is Spirit-filled, you may tell them about the Holy Spirit. If you were anything like me, you may have only heard about the Holy Spirit as you read or heard about certain chapters of the Bible. I think churches invest more in the youth because they are walking through a peer-pressured season. Community and friends have more impact on their life decisions sometimes than their families. We do need the Church to help speak truth and identity into our youth, and it helps reinforce what families need and believe. Don't get me wrong, I love youth ministry, and it had a huge impact on my life. Youth ministry is still something the Church needs to invest in. My problem is churches hire a youth pastor, but most churches run their children's ministry through volunteers. Even the point lead is usually a volunteer or the pastor's wife. Again, there is nothing wrong with this model, but what we need to point out is the focus and emphasis in youth ministry should not be the only point of focus. We should start pursuing children from the beginning.

In some cultures, like the Jewish culture for example, the rightful age of passage is twelve years of age. This is because these cultures believe that at this age a person is responsible for establishing what he believes and wants for his life. In fact, in some cultures, twelve-year-olds are considered mature and responsible enough even to live on their own and get married. Developmentally at the age of twelve, you will begin to decide what is real and not real and what you believe. Twelve-year-olds start cementing their independence from their parents, establishing core values, and questioning their parents' beliefs. It is a pivotal time in a life where children start laying down foundational beliefs. I wonder if this is why the Church pursues children heavily at this point. My belief is it can be too late, not too late for God of course, but why are we waiting? Why would we wait to pursue identity and establish truth, and not intentionally pursue and establish it earlier? God wants to meet us from the beginning. I think many children's ministries believe that they are establishing this foundation from the beginning. Maybe they are, but what I have seen and experienced is that we can do a whole lot better.

What if the Church established a strong foundation in our children from the beginning? That when our children entered youth ministry, they remained unwavering in the most pivotal time of their lives? What if our youth, from the very beginning, were able to stop the lies and put an end to their identity struggles associated with peer pressure? After all, as Fredrick Douglas said, "It is easier to build strong children than to repair broken men." And if we will help to establish a strong foundation in our children from the beginning, then when Christian children throughout the generations come up against adversity, they know confidently who they are in God and who God is. They, then, are equipped to face adversity in His wisdom, strength, and power.

Chapter 20

TRAINING YOUR TEAMS

Train up a child in the way he should go and
when he is old he will not depart from it.
—PROVERBS 22:6

THE BEST COMPLIMENT I WILL EVER RECEIVE IS WHEN A person is heartbroken over "having to" transition from serving in any capacity in the children's ministry at our church to some other adventure in their lives. This is one of the most common responses I receive from individuals serving with us in our ministry. We have found the value of people. Our teams are like family, and we work in an environment that builds each person into the best version of themselves. They leave heartbroken because watching children grow up in an environment fully empowered and championed to be great has been life-altering to them. The children's identity of who they are is built from the first moments they come into our doors, and that's what our teams have the privilege to participate in.

The other aspect that impacts our teams is the community of people who are committed to seeing a generation changed. There really is nothing else like it. I am still in contact with many people who have served alongside me and our teams, and they still remind me of how the time they spent with us changed and molded them into people who believe children can be taught, empowered, and transformed, and who also believe identity from Jesus should be instilled into children from the first moments and continue on as long as they are with us. Then a team member not only hears what we do with children, they see it with their own eyes become possible when children grab ahold of it and run passionately to the Father with bold faith. It is absolutely stunning! I will never get tired of seeing teams, parents, and children encounter the love of God or see others encounter the love of God and become changed—forever changed!

Children's ministry should not be a glorified daycare. Children's ministry needs volunteers who have a desire and passion to establish identity foundationally and functionally in our children. When I am referring to children's ministry, I am referencing the nursery as well. In other words, I'm talking about ages zero to twelve years. It's the whole blanket age before youth ministry.

The nursery is typically a safe, God-loving environment for our children so that we as adults can attend services and classes. It offers the same basic structures of a daycare with an emphasis of God. That is a great framework for structure, but I propose we need to make sure that we are creating a culture within that daycare. We need a culture that is reinforcing to our children who God is, who they are, and what God wants to do with their lives.

Culture by definition is a group or society of set social standards. The group has custom standards that express who it is and what it believes. I am proposing a culture that is a Kingdom culture or the culture of Heaven's perspective for humanity. It's what we saw Jesus come to this earth to do and what Jesus established with His disciples and the crowds around Him. This Kingdom culture in our children's ministry would be broken down to the fundamentals of who God is, who Christ is, who the Holy Spirit is, and who we are in Christ. A daycare ministry means we are meeting the basic needs of our children who are unable to care for themselves independently. Those are basically emotional and physical needs. Typically, churches will throw in some spiritual development that's achieved by using songs about God, coloring pages, and maybe a simple lesson plan about the Bible. This is a good start, but there is so much more. A Kingdom culture would help develop and establish a foundation of how spiritual development comes into play. It would actually practice real spiritual development.

For example, when we tell children the Holy Spirit is our Counselor, we want to consider what we can do to help them experience this aspect of the Holy Spirit. For me as a child, I knew about the Spirit being our Counselor, but I did not know what this meant practically. To me, the Holy Spirit was a character in the Bible who would hover, speak, move, or serve as a symbol. I never had a personal connection with the Holy Spirit or knew how He actually related to me as Counselor.

We have to get away from just telling the children about God, Jesus, and the Holy Spirit. We must move toward their having a real-life connection with the Trinity for themselves.

The Kingdom culture we establish in our rooms focuses on our identity and the identity of God to us. What does it mean to have God in our lives? What does it look like to have God in our lives? How does it feel to have God in our lives? What do we do with God in our lives? Some of the practices of Kingdom culture in our classrooms are as follows: (1) God is good, and He made us and He loves us; (2) with God, nothing in our lives is impossible for Him; (3) Jesus died so we could be with God for eternity; and (4) we were made with significance and are important to God.

We will get into the practicalities of how to incorporate this culture into your life. What you believe about children and what is possible will come out. If you believe children's ministry is a place to watch and care for them, then that is the product you will develop. If you believe in God and you believe He can speak and move among any person at any age or stage of life, then that allows God to move because you have faith for it. God honors our faith. If you recall, the centurion came to Jesus with a faith Jesus had never seen before, and Jesus was pleased with the centurion's faith. The same value of faith was with the woman with the issue of blood who was healed. She just believed if she touched Jesus' robe she would be healed of a medical condition with which she had suffered for twelve years. Jesus pointed out to everyone that it was her faith that healed her. This is the very reason we have God's Word to impart the principles that we are to live by. Your children can and will do great things in their lives because Jesus has given *all* of us this truth. If you believe it, then you have set the standard of your faith. Your children will now have a foundation of faith to stand upon.

The vision of our ministry comes from Proverbs 22:6, *"Train up a child in the way he should go and when he is old he will not depart from it."* We train up a child by imparting, equipping, guiding, parenting through experience, teaching curriculum, and developing relationship with them. We train them that, from this point forward, they are to seek, find, and follow after their loving Father God to know their identity, calling, and destiny in and from God. And when they become mature and strengthened, they will then become fathers, mothers, and leaders for the future generations. And this helps keep this culture an ecosystem in design. Once they have experienced a personal loving relationship with God their Father, revival and renewal will continue. The next generations will produce this ongoing fruit.

It is our heart to equip and release children, through the impartation and demonstration of God's manifest presence, to usher in the Kingdom of Heaven which brings this cultural transformation.

Practically, this looks like teaching and imparting. By teaching, we show, instruct, guide, and train. By imparting, we make known, communicate knowledge, give, bestow, and share. Our children must not just hear about a loving Father, but they have to experience a loving Father for themselves, imparting not only a knowledge but adding an experience of who He is. When we create a space for our children to hear and experience this for themselves, they are also seeing it in peers around them.

Practically, we will teach the children to worship, pray, believe for the impossible things, talk about things God is doing and has done, speak identity and truth over themselves and others, read and know God's Word, and learn to hear His voice and experience Him. We do this all while caring for their emotional and physical needs in a loving and caring environment. This is a training ground to equip a generation of children who will change the world in which they live.

In order to help create a Kingdom culture within your classroom or environment, you will need to find a team who shares the same vision and heart. I have found that, when I share my vision and heart for children's ministry, I can easily tell if another individual is able to help serve and add to this vision. I refuse to find someone just to fill a spot in a room or on our team in order to meet our basic needs. Honestly, children's ministry is filled mostly with these individuals. I do, however, think these individuals need to be inspired and empowered to deposit a part of themselves into the lives of children. Often, these individuals are merely babysitting. I have found, if I communicate that I need each person to deposit something valuable and impactful into the lives of each child they will minister to, then they are up for the challenge. Sometimes, I may need to pour into the team because they are unsure where to start. If they are willing to grow and partner with me, then I am willing to help build people.

Once you have the team, the environment will become full and life-giving with each person feeling valued and empowered to impart or contribute to this beautiful environment. I do not expect perfection, and neither should you. In fact, we are all on a journey to learn and grow, and with that comes mistakes. I am not afraid of mistakes, but I am more afraid of performance and perfection. Mistakes are how we learn and grow, and mistakes are expected. Find people who are willing to be authentic and real yet value you as a leader.

Once you have shared your vision and heart with your team, you will need to create clear expectations of them while they serve in ministry. If they know what you need and what you value, then this will give them space to deposit themselves into your ministry. An empowered individual is such an inspirational person. Just as we are growing our children, remember it is a great time to know we can grow our teams. As Bill Johnson has said, "I am not interested in building big ministries, but I am interested in building big people."

I know that, if you create such a value for your children and for your team, you will find your rooms are thriving instead of just surviving. So many times, my team has come to me in tears because they needed to leave their role for whatever reason. They were sad to leave because theirs has been the most incredible experience and job they have ever had. They have enjoyed this season of their lives when they felt alive and felt the value that they put into the lives of the children. They were marked by the season, receiving ministry from it themselves. Little did they know that what they were giving was what they were also receiving. It is a gift to reap what you sow, and you will absolutely find this true when you pour out your heart and life into the future generations. I once had a team member tell me that this opportunity to serve had actually healed their own childhood. The person thanked me for creating a place to see and know what a fully-empowered environment looks like.

Imagine your team and children as individuals whom God has intended for greatness. If you cannot imagine this, then just speak as if they are until you believe it. If everyone would look at each child with the future destiny that God has for them, then we would pour into them very differently. If you looked at a child and knew they would be the next Bill Johnson, President of the United States, missionary, mother, or school janitor, you should pour all you can into that child. No matter the calling on their lives, they were designed for greatness to change the world. Each person was formed and knitted together in their mother's womb, and the Lord was the Master Designer and Crafter of each being. His time and intention on each person can only be for greatness. We are to reflect the One who made us in His own image.

Chapter 21

EVERYONE HAS A PLACE

*Jesus said, "Let the little children come
to me, and do not forbid them; for of
such is the kingdom of heaven."*
—MATTHEW 19:14

I REMEMBER A TIME WHEN WE HAD A FAMILY COME INTO the hallway of our children's ministry to check in their children just because we had a class for special needs children. We not only had unsaved families come to church because we offered a class, we also had families move across the world to bring their special needs children to our classes for children with special needs. The first family I mentioned came because there was a space for their child on a Sunday morning, and they were looking for help and a break. The second category I mentioned happens all the time where people come to bring their children to us because they have heard about our classes and they have heard that children have been healed. There are countless stories of families traveling for a few hours to days just to get their children into a place where their children can receive ministry and learn to minister. This is what the Body of Christ is all about—every part has a purpose and function.

When I think of Jesus, I think of home. I can't imagine a life without Him, and I never want to even try. To know that there are people trying to live a life without the love and relationship of Jesus is really mind baffling. I know that, if they met Him, they would see He can and will change everything for the better in their lives. Jesus shows us what the Church gets to do. In Matthew 19, we see a part of what the Church with the heart of Jesus gets to do. He calls everyone to Himself, even to the point that it can offend others. I don't really believe Jesus is in the business of offending people because that is not who He is. The people are the ones who choose offense.

We humans have some kind of codebook that we create. This codebook could be inherited from our upbringing and even culture. We can even interpret our codebook incorrectly from the original codebook from God—His Word. For some reason, society has placed a lesser value on children than adults. We can go back and forth on why or how we have arrived at this, but it does not seem to be a new issue. We know that men have been ascribed more value than children and women back in biblical days and even today. Jesus actually had to say aloud to His disciples—to the ones who were rebuking those who brought the children to Jesus—to let the children come to Him. Jesus came into our world to bring clarity and life to places where we misrepresented the original purpose and design of Kingdom culture. I am wondering how many of us are living within our own codebooks and do not realize that children have a big part to play in the Kingdom of Heaven as well as adults. I did a quick search and found that children are mentioned over 300 times in the Bible. There is such an importance and emphasis on children, and it is God's heart that they be seen and heard.

One of the most impactful things I believe my parents did for me and my brothers when we were young was they found a church that first had a great children's ministry and youth group. They did not go somewhere to meet their own needs. In fact, they were willing to get less out of church so that we could get something more. I am so grateful that they found a place that really pursued our hearts as children and connected us to the heart of our Heavenly Father.

Our churches are filled with families. However, I am aware that they are filled with more than families. The emphasis that I feel called to though is to be the voice to put weight and value and worth on our children. If we did not have our children and families, our congregations would most likely not live beyond one to two generations. If you are looking at sustaining revival and life in the Church, then you need to put some emphasis on children, and I would propose more than just youth ministry.

Church is a place where we can come and rest, be known, be in community, be challenged, grow, and so much more. I see church as a place where families gather. No matter what part of the family stage you are in, you are a part of a greater family. In the family, there is space for each person, and church should have this space as well. Each person has a name, a place, and a role. This name, place, and role can change through the course of life, but there should always be a place for every stage of life. I have always pictured church like a home, probably because to me church was a second home. In a home, there are different spaces and rooms with different functions. The same can be said for church. I am going to walk through what I can see and envision for each space of a home and how this can relate to church itself.

Every home should have a porch or entry from the outside. The porch is a focal point to enter the home, and you should have a starting place for entry. This space can be attractive and grand, but it can also be worn down or hard to find. Whatever phase your church is in, the original design and purpose should draw people into your church. We all want to find a place where we are welcomed and want to be. People coming to a whole and healthy home should be greeted by a sign at the doormat that says, "Welcome." This is a beautiful reminder of how valuable it is to see people and welcome them in. As anyone would enter the front door of a home, they should be greeted with love and joy.

The next space in the home would be a living room. This room has the most frequent gathering space in the home. It's the place where most of life happens. From guests to family, it is a natural place for everyone to gather.

Then you have the kitchen which is the heart of a home. This space is for nourishment and comfort to anyone in the home. You come into this space to be fed, to break bread together, to grow in comfort and strength.

Bedrooms are rooms for individual life. This could be stages of life, maybe a space for personal growth in the season of life you are in. You could have a guest room for people who visit, a room for children with age-appropriate furniture and items, a parent's room that can be a place for vulnerability and intimacy.

Lastly, you would have a bathroom. This space is a very personal space for caring for your personal needs and cleansing. You come here daily to maintain cleanliness and rid yourself of dirt or waste.

I believe churches have all these "home" spaces in their buildings. Everyone should have a space where they belong and are welcome. There are often times in your life where each space in a home is more focal to your respective stage in life. A whole family and community can gather in one home and receive different life experiences due to the stages of life they are in. It is one roof that can cover a home for an entire family and community.

A child has just as much space and freedom to belong as an adult does. A child's space would look different than an adult's space because it would cater to their needs or stage in life. Remember the bedrooms in the home I described earlier. The child's space should be welcoming to them just as much as a similar space would be welcoming to an adult. There are many factors in creating a space and environment for a child or anyone for that matter. The physical space is just one important factor. The people, the culture, and how you welcome a child are other important factors. The focal point should be how do you make a person feel seen, known, valued, and important. You and your team should really break down what it means to make children and their families experience that they are important in your ministry. This is not just about a space but about the heart and environment that you are creating. A child is about one-fourth of your church ministry. If you realize a child is connected to another fourth of your church, then in essence a child is half of your church congregation. The child comes with an adult. That adult is the parent, grandparent, aunt, uncle, guardian, foster parent, friend, or neighbor. Ministries in the church are all important because we are ministering to people no matter their age, sex, or stage in life. This is whom the Church is called to—people.

Jesus shows us the value of the one—the value in a widow, a child, a very rich man, the religious, the outcast, the lost, the sinner, and so on. The Church gets to give value to people. The reason people come into the house of God or a community of believers is because they are there to encounter the love of Jesus, to experience His presence. We come to worship, to find Him, to pray, to lean into His arms, and to find comfort and truth in His Word. Matthew 18:20 says, *"For where two or three gather in my name, there am I with them."* When God is with us, no one can be against us. We gather together to find Him, hear Him, watch Him, and worship Him. This is the highest point of value for our human existence—to come to our Creator and find Him.

So, when anyone walks into a house of God, no one is excluded. Every person gathered in the name of Jesus together needs to know that God is with them. It is one thing to think this thought. It is nice and comforting, and I believe we all think about this. The difference is that we need to believe this very truth. God the Creator of Heaven and Earth, the Author and Finisher, the One who holds existence, the One who is the Beginning and the End is *with us!* He wants to be with us, not apart from us. He delights to give love and life to us. His love is so big that He was willing to give up His Son. I don't know about you, but if I just sit in this one thought for the rest of my life, there should never be a day that I don't get transformed and my life left unaffected by this thought. *You* are what He wants. The church building is just a place to put an "X" on a location where we come to have *God* come and dwell with us.

The church is a place where He is asking us to *abide* with Him. I must clarify that the church is not the only place where we get to abide with Him. We get to find Him and sit with Him every moment of every day anywhere we go. It is not a place; it is a posture of our minds, hearts, and attention to Him. This word *abiding* has been changing my perspective in life. Did you know that one of the main definitions of abiding is, "continuing for a long time"? This is what I want to do. I want to stay in a place continuing to be with God for a very long time. In essence, this is eternal in its very design. The reason we abide with Him is to receive sustainable life. God's Word says we come to abide because it produces fruit; in fact, we can't bear fruit without abiding (see John 15:4). Abiding is our salvation (see 2 John 1:9). In abiding with God comes His Word, His anointing, His presence, His life, His promises, and so much more. We are called to constantly abide in Him. The definition of "continuing" means it comes with a responsibility to keep moving forward, to always press in and not to stop. It is always ongoing. It is a state of being and not just an action. To me this is another reason we come and gather at church. We are all abiding, but we are commonly gathered for the same vision. We are there for *Him*. Then if we are there for Him, and He is with us, and especially more confidently when we call on His name, then we must remember that *every* person plays a part in the church.

I grew up with a brother who we adopted out of foster care. He came into our family's life when he was six weeks old as a foster child. He came into our lives and never left our family. He was born with fetal alcohol syndrome and a twisted spine. He was not very responsive, and eventually he was diagnosed with severe autism. For the most, he was non-verbal. His verbal communication consisted and still consists of that of an eighteen-month-old to two-year-old: one-word communication that is not perfectly formulated. He is a beautiful person, and he taught and continues to teach me so much about God and people. His life, though, meant that he didn't look, act, or really fit into our normal world. So, my brother could not stand being in a room full of people or sound. He had to figure out how to manage in the normal world that we had around us. Noise was a huge hindrance to his functioning. He had to wear earplugs and not just normal earplugs. He found the swimmers wax that swimmers put in their ears to protect themselves from getting swimmers' ear. And even that was not enough. He had to put that wax in his ears, and then wear earmuffs designed to protect people from gun noise. When my brother was young, these were the only kind of earmuffs we could find. Now there are wonderful noise-cancelling headphones that are found everywhere. If my brother did not have this double level of noise cancelation, then he would throw a tantrum that looked like he could crawl out of his skin. He would have tears streaming down his face, and he would inflict pain on himself, which I believe was to distract himself from the noise that pierced his ears.

My family attended church two to three days a week, and we had to prepare my brother for it. When we entered church, my brother had to stay with my parents the whole time. One of the simple reasons was there was no one to care for him with his special needs. Another reason was because it was easier for my parents to just keep him with us. I think my parents did well considering the circumstances, and their heart was always intended to care for him. They never expected anyone to care for him other than themselves. I think it was because they chose my brother to be their child and promised to care for and protect him. My parents' value for a covenant relationship was strong. When they said *yes* to him, it was a *yes* with no end in sight. So, when they told the judge that they would care for my brother, they really knew what that meant. If there had been a team then and or a facility to care for my brother to learn and thrive in church, it would have been revolutionary over thirty-five years ago. The church is a place for everyone to thrive, grow, and learn.

What I saw the school provide my brother in comparison to what church offered was mind blowing. I never expected church to offer the same level of care, but I wondered what it would look like to offer just as much care and design for children who needed some alteration to their environments to thrive. I mean, the schools were light years ahead of us in church. They had funding, but we had and have heart, and we have people who want to lay down their lives to serve God. There had to be something we could do. We can and are able to look around us and can find incredible people in our communities. Not only are these people who are in our communities very incredible, but they are extremely gifted in some specific areas. This is the Body, and this is the design of the Body.

What would it look like to look around our community of people and find out who we have in our midst? What would our houses of worship look like? What would our cities look like? We have some amazing and talented people all around us who are doing life with us. They may not all be willing to serve, but when you cast vision, heart, value, and some testimonies of what God can do, people will be moved to sign up, even if it is for a short season. You will have those loyal people who serve for many seasons, and all of these together will cause the Body to thrive. You have an abundance of what you tolerate. That statement is not bad necessarily. It can be the most encouraging statement you may hear. Let me tell you why. If you have an abundance of joy, it is because you are tolerating joy. You can also have an abundance of complaining and grumbling because you have a high tolerance for them. It is just that simple. It is what you are willing to tolerate.

ABOUT AMY GAGNON

Amy Gagnon is the director of children's ministry and on the church leadership team of Bethel Church. She and her husband, Jeremy, have four daughters, and have been at Bethel Church for over 25 years. They will be moving to Greenville, South Carolina, to plant Studio Church as the Children's and Family life pastor. Amy has an insatiable hunger to see children reach their full potential in Christ. She also has a passion for spiritually healthy families living out revival in their homes in practical ways.

Connect with Amy on
Instagram:Amygagnon76
Facebook: Amy Burgar Gagnon

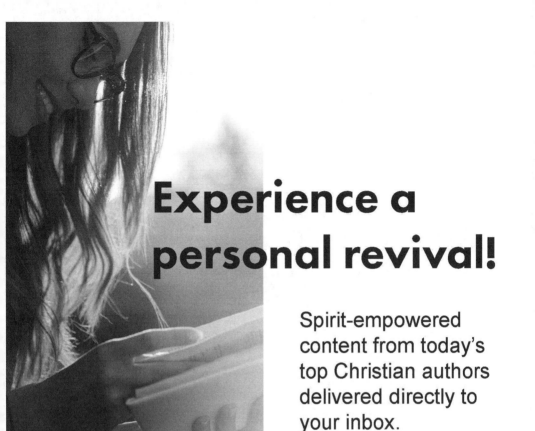